THE RUGBY CLUBS OF WALES

THE
RUGBY CLUBS
OF WALES

David Parry-Jones

STANLEY PAUL

London Sydney Auckland Johannesburg

Stanley Paul & Co. Ltd

An imprint of Century Hutchinson Ltd

62–65 Chandos Place, London WC2N 4NW

Century Hutchinson Australia (Pty) Ltd
20 Alfred Street, Milsons Point, Sydney 2061

Century Hutchinson New Zealand Limited
PO Box 40–086, Glenfield, Auckland 10

Century Hutchinson South Africa (Pty) Ltd
PO Box 337, Bergvlei 2012, South Africa

First published 1989

Set in Century Old Style by Bookworm Typesetting, Manchester

Printed and bound in Great Britain by
Butler & Tanner Ltd, Frome and London

British Library Cataloguing in Publication Data
Parry – Jones, David
The rugby clubs of Wales.
1. Wales. Rugby Union Football to 1988
I. Title
796.33′3′09429

ISBN 0 09 173850 4

Photo acknowledgement
The author and publishers would like to thank Colorsport, John Harris and Bob Thomas for permission to
reproduce their copyright photographs.

CONTENTS

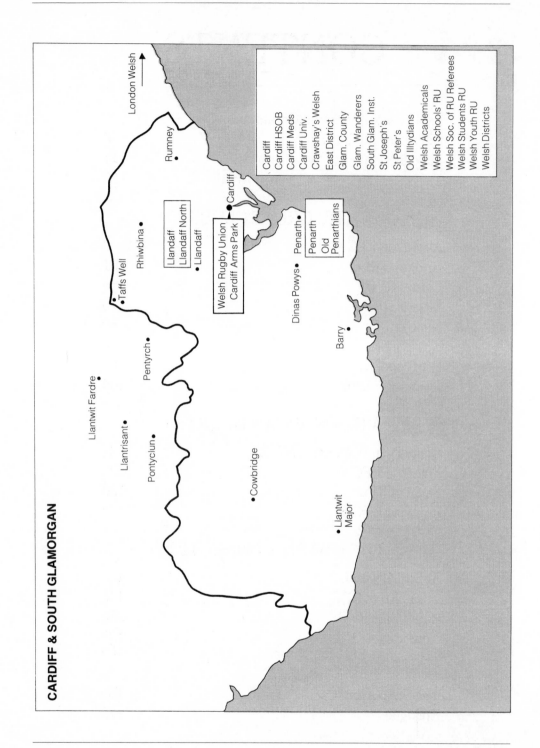

CARDIFF & SOUTH GLAMORGAN

London Welsh

Rumney

Rhiwbina

Taffs Well

Pentyrch

Llantwit Fardre

Llantrisant

Pontyclun

Cowbridge

Llantwit Major

Dinas Powys

Barry

Cardiff

Penarth

Llandaff
Llandaff North
Llandaff

Welsh Rugby Union
Cardiff Arms Park

Penarth
Old
Penarthians

Cardiff
Cardiff HSOB
Cardiff Meds
Cardiff Univ.
Crawshay's Welsh
East District
Glam. County
Glam. Wanderers
South Glam. Inst.
St Joseph's
St Peter's
Old Illtydians
Welsh Academicals
Welsh Schools' RU
Welsh Soc. of RU Referees
Welsh Students RU
Welsh Youth RU
Welsh Districts

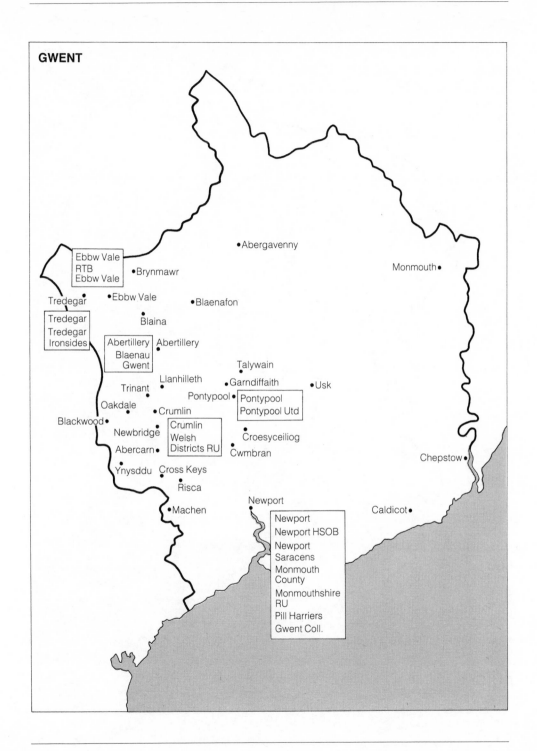

GWENT

Ebbw Vale
RTB
Ebbw Vale
•Brynmawr
•Abergavenny
Monmouth•

Tredegar•
•Ebbw Vale
•Blaenafon

Tredegar
Tredegar
Ironsides

Blaina

Abertillery
Blaenau
Gwent
Abertillery

Talywain

Llanhilleth
•Garndiffaith
•Usk

Trinant•
Pontypool•
Pontypool
Pontypool Utd

Oakdale•

Blackwood•
•Crumlin

Newbridge•
Crumlin
Welsh
Districts RU
•Croesyceiliog

Abercarn•
Cwmbran

Ynysddu•
Cross Keys

Risca

•Machen
Newport•
Caldicot•

Chepstow•

Newport
Newport HSOB
Newport
Saracens
Monmouth
County
Monmouthshire
RU
Pill Harriers
Gwent Coll.

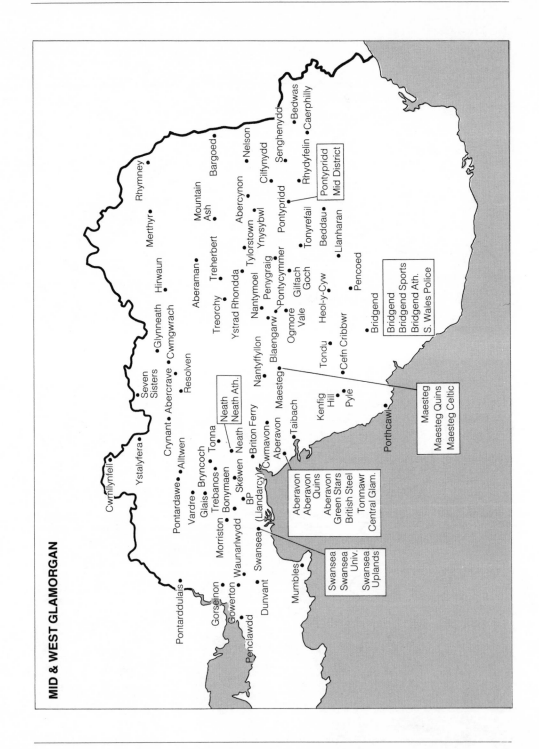

MID & WEST GLAMORGAN

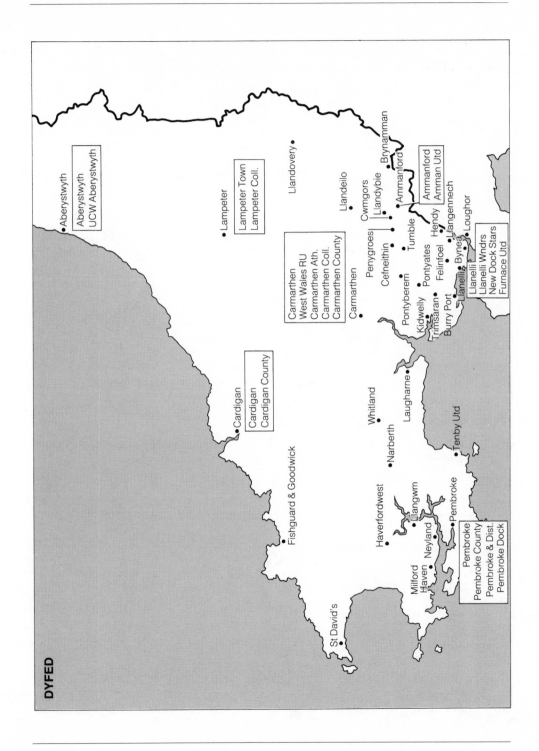

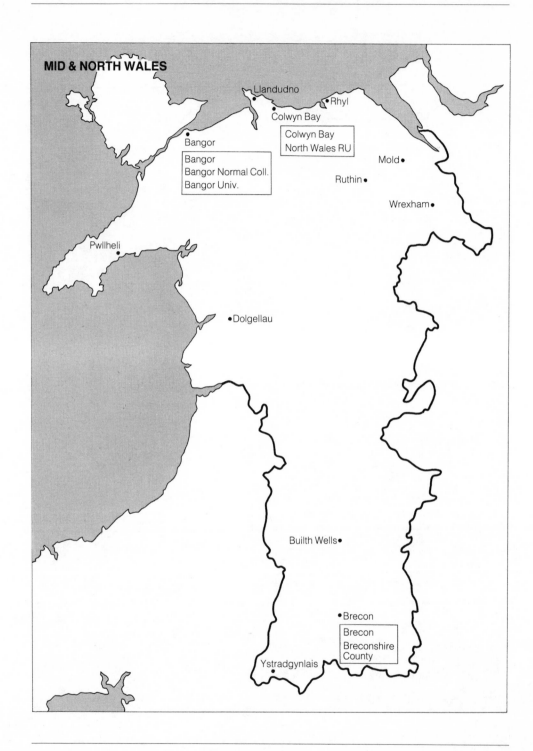

MID & NORTH WALES

Llandudno

Rhyl

Colwyn Bay

Colwyn Bay
North Wales RU

Bangor

Bangor
Bangor Normal Coll.
Bangor Univ.

Mold

Ruthin

Wrexham

Pwllheli

Dolgellau

Builth Wells

Brecon

Brecon
Breconshire
County

Ystradgynlais

INTRODUCTION

All things to all men

After-dinner speeches at post-International match functions are usually bland orations. A captain's prime duty is to thank the referees and touch judges. If victorious, he pays tribute to the strenuous efforts of his players and commiserates with the losers. If beaten, he congratulates the opposition and promises to do better next year. Urbanity is the order of the evening.

Guests at the celebration banquet at Cardiff's Angel Hotel after the match between Wales and England on 18 March 1989 could therefore scarcely believe their ears when the Welsh skipper, Paul Thorburn, delivered a calculated insult to a leading London Rugby critic and invited him to leave the room. The victim's offence had been to pen, a few days before the match, an article suggesting that it might be healthy for the game in the Principality were the Welsh team to lose. Once the normally well-balanced, personable Thorburn has more experience of captaincy and the responses which are normally made on such occasions he will doubtless regret his outburst – which possibly cost him a place with the British Isles party which toured Australia in the summer of 1989.

When the story broke in the Welsh Press on the Monday morning, however, (and was taken up by the media everywhere) the considered reaction of many readers was that the Thorburn polemic really represented the tip of a volcano which had been rumbling ominously for the best part of two years, if not for a decade. Just below the surface of Welsh Rugby football smouldered fires of tumult and dissent of an unprecedented intensity, fanned by gusts of argument and anger. Thorburn's words were simply the lava that finally erupted.

His team, and those captained by Richard Moriarty, Bleddyn Bowen and Jonathan Davies before him, deserved the stick they had been dealt by the media. Even though they finally took third place in the tournament, the World Cup campaign of 1987 contained the biggest-ever thrashing suffered by Wales in the twentieth century, a 49–6 defeat by New Zealand at the semi-final stage. Temporary elation over a somewhat fortunate Triple Crown in the following winter's Five Nations tournament was doused by France's victory at Cardiff in the Grand Slam decider and, in the summer, two more devastating defeats at the hands of the All Blacks by 52–3 and 54–9. The shell-shocked Welsh returned home, replaced their coach, re-shaped their team – and promptly continued a sad sequence of surrenders to Romania, Scotland, Ireland and, again, France. An unprecedented four-match whitewash stared them in the face until the last-ditch win over England which stemmed the tide of defeat.

It is significant that Thorburn's controversial remarks were made by a victorious, not a losing, captain. Despite an opportunity to be magnanimous towards critics who had dismissed Wales's chances, he still fired from the hip. He probably made sure that the big, cleansing debate which Rugby in Wales certainly needs would at last take place. There is much to be said; many reforms are needed. The Welsh need rousing from the Big Sleep in which they have basked since the golden days of the 'seventies.

Rugby Football in Wales may be just a game, but it is all things to all people.

There are those who look on from a distance. Such people seldom if ever watch Cardiff play Newport or Llanelli versus Neath. On a winter Saturday afternoon they go shopping, play Bingo, watch the Film on Two, or see Swansea City play Wrexham. Four or five times a year, however, when the National XV is at play, they suddenly discover a huge involvement. They anxiously demand to know from the cognoscenti what the result is likely to be, question the ability of a wing who is about to win his first cap – and even put out feelers for North Stand tickets. They are an undercurrent of pride and passion streaming just below the surface – but their concern is less about Welsh Rugby than about the broader reputation of Wales itself.

Closer to events are the grass roots supporters. Such men, and women, will never win caps and may never even play a game of Rugby, let alone appear in a major fixture. They are the fans who talk endlessly about matches past and matches to come; about great and not-so-great players; about tours and trips; about match-winning tries, phenomenal penalty goals and intricate statistics. They are the folk who support Llanharan in the rain, cut sandwiches for the teams, pull pints in the bar, wash jerseys – and who will throng the East Terrace on big match day. They are the homespun critics who bash the ear of players and Press, submit edited TV highlights to ceaseless debate, and display astonishing erudition at club quiz nights. The more eloquent of their number make hilarious after-dinner speeches or exploit Rugby football in a kindly way on stage or in pantomime. They may or may not be great patriots – but they care tremendously about Welsh Rugby, because it is their obsession.

Then there are the Press and media representatives. Nine out of every ten of their number write or broadcast about Rugby from a deep love of the game and a desire to promote and extol it – many are past players of standing. Their task ranges from the accurate recording of matches and results through to in-depth analysis of preparation and tactics; from shivering reportage on a January evening somewhere along the Heads of the Valleys to commentating on a showpiece International match at Cardiff Arms Park. Other sectors of the Rugby public in Wales often misunderstand their motives and aims: but they constitute a reasonably true mirror of the generality of spectators, and often their praise is more generous – and their criticism less acid – than the verbal missives hurled from grandstands and terraces. It is the critic's lot that players, being young and only human, lap up compliments and love to have their great deeds written up or replayed on screen; if, however, they are criticised or depicted in an unfavourable light the following Saturday, they are quick to sulk or grip the offender warmly by the throat.

Administrators are the engine room that propels Welsh Rugby's colourful cavalcade smoothly along the rails. Whether as coaches to Extra B fifteens or members of the Welsh Rugby Union's general committee, such men gain a deep fulfilment from their work. It is noble, and unpaid; and it generally goes unacknowledged. Young players often do not even know who is the secretary of their club let alone the names of those who arrange fixtures, clean changing rooms, see to the care of the pitch, book transport, keep the books and run the bar. At a more exalted level, elected Representatives must spend many an evening with clubs in their Districts, lending a sympathetic ear to complaints and assessing drifts of opinion. In exchange for the time and effort they put in, why should not such servants of the game go on trips with the National team, sit down to free dinners and enjoy the multitude of free pints that are pressed upon them?

Into this category fall selectors – the 'Big Five' – coaches and referees. They, in particular, find themselves in a no-win situation: if a game flows, the players are praised; if play is stop-go, the referee is to blame. If the National XV does well, this is wholly to the credit of its members; if it fails, coaches and selectors are sure to be blamed. Bystanders blasting them with abuse too readily forget that these vital cogs in the machine are unpaid, and do not have to take the flak. Administrating or refereeing is their amateur sport, too.

And there are the players, perhaps ten or twelve thousand in Wales. All but a select few take the field every Saturday for fun bent chiefly on exercise and the working-up of a thirst. Fresh out of offices, factories and company cars they have steam to let off – for few today are engaged in the traditional heavy industries once dominant in the Principality. For them, Rugby offers the best possible chance of exercising limbs, flexing muscles, testing stamina, co-operating closely with team-mates, and attempting to deceive an opponent by running past him with the ball. This is a formidable array of sporting skills, offering to participants a measure of satisfaction deriving precisely from the amount of effort they choose to put into their game. At so unpretentious a level, glory or pride scarcely comes into it: just the pleasure to be derived from vigorous exercise.

Club and representative Rugby at its highest levels in Wales demands a more complex response. Here much motivation also stems from a desire for physical engagement in a competitive situation. The player who opts for a first-class club, however, thereby ensuring that he will be watched by the national selectors, accepts the rewards and the penalties of playing in front of big crowds for whom he represents their town or country. If he is adequate, if he is good, if he is supreme, he will have the cheers of spectators ringing constantly in his ears. If he makes costly errors, he may be jeered and abused; and when he is dropped the Press will broadcast the news to the world at large. Fame is a spur whose point is very sharp.

This book looks at the way in which these disparate elements cohere into the complex and volatile structure which is Welsh Rugby. It considers the great clubs, the second rank, and the so-called junior clubs who bid for glory in local leagues or the Schweppes Cup competition. It looks at outstanding players of the past and present, and recalls games which thrilled thousands. And it asks whether the game in Wales possesses the verve and resilience to advance confidently into the twenty-first century.

For some suggest that its days as a front-rank sport in the Principality are numbered. It is indeed beset by problems.

Slings and arrows

Wales's status in world Rugby belies her size. The total population is below three million; the game's hotbed lies within a southern hinterland some seventy miles in length by twenty-five broad. From this narrow base, nevertheless, there have emerged clubs, teams and players able to hold their own with any opponents. In the ten decades since their first International victory of 1884 against Ireland, the Welsh have registered more victories in European competition than any of their

Five Nations rivals, have beaten New Zealand three times, and given mighty South Africa some tremendous tussles. Clubs have successfully seen off challenges from major touring teams. British Isles sides have regularly included a substantial Welsh complement. There has been innovation; there has been imaginative administration; and recent years have seen the construction of a magnificent, purpose-built stadium whose facilities are unsurpassed.

And the Welsh have provided marvellous entertainment, fresh in the memory of the senior generation. The 'seventies saw the emergence of a crop of players whose presence would have enhanced any team in the history of Rugby Football. Three Grand Slams and five Triple Crowns came Wales's way when great men like Edwards, John, Gerald and Mervyn Davies, Bennett and J.P.R. Williams ruled the roost (with occasional interruptions from the All Blacks). Supporters perspired their way through a heady Rugby fever that lasted for a whole decade.

When the last of the superstars hung up his boots the Welsh Rugby public, its ego boosted by a constant fix of victory and triumph, fell victim to severe and chronic withdrawal symptoms. Able though the new players were, they could not guarantee to produce the magic or the winning touch possessed by their predecessors. Cardiff Arms Park, for long an impregnable citadel, became a venue where most visiting countries were in with a chance. In the 'seventies, some had said perversely that it would do the 'arrogant' Welsh good to lose a few games (nobody ever hears New Zealanders voicing such sentiments). The reality was less agreeable.

Disillusionment thus replaced jubilation as the dominant mood. The National XV stumbled from defeat to defeat and slid steadily down the world-wide table of merit, with only sporadic reminders of bygone greatness. The stream of outstanding players shrank to a trickle and those who did emerge were often lured away to the professional ranks. Rugby League has always been a thorn in the flesh of the amateur game in Wales; and in an indifferent period defections by men of the calibre of Terry Holmes, Stuart Evans, David Bishop and Jonathan Davies were cruel blows. Some would argue that harsh pruning encourages a plant to grow; but no right-minded gardener cuts off a bloom in its prime.

Television and the Press were not slow to underline the growing crisis. Reporters and broadcasters searched their vocabularies for adjectives and epithets to describe the clouds of crisis that had slowly gathered over the game. Screaming headlines appeared about 'tinpot armies', 'Welsh Wallies' and 'Darkest Hours'. Media interviews were characterised by aggression and anxiety.

Undoubtedly criticism hurts amateur players, who do not have weekly wage packets to console them for harsh words which they may read about themselves. In contrast to the genial relationships between reporters and players of the previous decade, the 'eighties brought bitter feuds between leading Internationals and Rugby Pressmen. Often, ante-rooms outside post-match dinners were the scene of angry confrontations in which voices were raised and fingers jabbed at chests. Some players declined to speak to certain reporters. Undoubtedly the on-field lobby would describe the media as one of the principal problems affecting the running and playing of the game.

But the media have a job to do, and speaking the truth is part of a reporter's job. From time to time this is bound to involve saying that a match was lousy, that a player had a disastrous game or that a selector should call it a day. Sometimes it is necessary to scrutinise the Laws of the game and see how current conduct squares with them, whether in the context of thuggery on the pitch or adherence to the amateur code. And besides celebrating success, the honest critic has to look at failure and state the reasons for it, as he sees them. Such passing of opinion may be controversial, but it is valid. It may appear in 100,000 copies of a newspaper, or be broadcast to an audience measured in millions; but only in that sense is it any different from, or more or less useful, than a view expressed in the club bar after a match. The Press are sometimes exhorted by players and selectors to 'get behind us'; but that is the job of supporters, not critics.

It should be borne in mind, too, that stinging criticism is often the goad which extracts a better performance from a side or a player in the next match. Nothing fires up a team more than being written off as inept no-hopers of limited ability. Such previews are often – rightly – pasted up in changing rooms before the kick-off.

And finally, media-men really do prefer to write and talk about winning teams. For them victory for Wales gives an opportunity to indulge a touch of purple prose rather than knocking copy. Though they preserve a strict impartiality while assessing events, they too can be counted among the patriots.

Among the prime targets of public criticism both in the media and elsewhere in recent years has been the Welsh Rugby Union itself. If this body strikes people as amorphous and without personality, that is probably the WRU's own fault. For reasons best known to itself it has cultivated a low profile, epitomised in its failure, despite prompting, to appoint a Press officer whose task would be to address the wider world on the issues which confront it. The Secretary speaks from time to time, but other commitments clearly make it impossible for him to be at the media's beck and call.

In some ways, the WRU is deliberately and perversely a non-communicator. Perhaps the most exciting and eagerly-awaited announcements to emerge from its Cardiff Arms Park headquarters each winter are the names of the successive teams chosen to represent Wales in the Five Nations Championship. These bulletins, however, are delivered perfunctorily in the shape of a simple team list, with perhaps the curt addendum that so-and-so was not considered because of doubts over his fitness. The selectors do not readily make themselves or a spokesman available to answer the burning questions that often arise: why a certain player has been dropped, or picked, or why the captaincy has changed hands. Yet the reasoning process and the arguments leading to a team selection are of burning interest to those who will be paying spectators at the forthcoming match or will watch it avidly on television. Chairmen of selectors take refuge in 'no comment' statements, or have even been heard to admonish reporters, 'I'm surprised you should ask me that.'

A side-issue here is the extraordinary ban on media interviews which the Union attempts to impose upon members of the National squad with the exception of the captain and new caps (without, that is, their being arranged via a cumbersome and time-consuming 'official channel'). Such men are not invariably the sole objects of interest in the build-up to a representative match. Writers and broadcasters find it frustrating not to be able to contact players freely and without delay. This is particularly irritating for contributors to daily newspapers, who have deadlines to meet and cannot readily wait to be rung back, maybe hours later, with permission to telephone their man.

This stricture, probably unique in the democratised world, has no parallel in other Rugby playing countries where participants talk without hindrance to reporters and broadcasters. In Wales it was originally imposed during the 'seventies when pressure on the stars was intense. Now, it is surely out-dated. Other considerations apart, it robs players of the chance to give interviews which would certainly be interesting – and harmless – and which would please them and their families and admirers.

There is a body of opinion – it includes at least one former Secretary – which holds that the Union, in particular its general committee, is too large and unwieldy. Its thirty-four members, who meet monthly, inevitably spend much of the time wading through minutiae – approval of Minutes alone can be very time-consuming.

If the general committee were a smaller body, this might be a speedier process; but an oligarchy is by nature slow to initiate radical surgery upon itself. In the circumstances, therefore, whether the WRU can lift its head from the paperwork on the table and take a more visionary view of the way ahead remains a matter of opinion.

At the time of Ray Williams's resignation as Secretary, for example, many thought the moment had arrived to review the way in which the Union was administrated. They argued keenly that the post of Secretary should be up-graded to that of Chief Executive with a far more positive role; and that a marketing officer should be appointed to deal with active promotion of the game in Wales and negotiate sponsorship. It is relevant that the annual 'take' from outside sources like sponsorship, television and advertising is now very close to gate receipts during an average International season.

Although the installation of the admirable David East, formerly Chief Constable of Glamorgan, was widely and warmly welcomed, the opportunity to make those structural changes was ignored; and the newcomer must for the time being undertake both the administrative and commercial chores of what has become an ever-expanding, multi-million pound business. A modest start on spreading the load has been made with the appointment of three regional development officers; but it is to be hoped that in due course the WRU will take a leaf out of Twickenham's book and hire a senior entrepreneurial figure to create and capitalise upon openings for marketing and promoting the game in Wales.

The other criticism concerns the make-up of the general committee. At present it comprises District Representatives, Schools and Youth delegates, and members from the Districts and London Welsh. With the exception of the last-named, these are not men engaged in the day-to-day running of gate-taking clubs. This is a factor which sticks in the gullet of the so-called 'Merit Table' group, whose seasonal competition is sponsored by Whitbread Wales. It has led to an on-going feud between Wales's leading clubs and the WRU, which has tended to relegate the general good of the game to second place. Fierce arguments about competitions, and specifically the introduction of a league structure, have been characterised by rancour and threaten to stand deadlocked.

The Merit Table clubs are a self-perpetuating body with a cautious and conservative outlook – and have not always been noted for realism or tact in their public utterances. It is hard to envisage radical reforms or innovations springing from within their ranks. To some extent they are seen as an elite, whose pre-eminence is self-styled and has not been won in competition. The fact is, however, that they are Welsh Rugby's battle fleet, containing the toughest armour and the biggest guns. They attract crowds who pay good money to watch them play; they have the strongest fixture lists; they keep the game in the news; and the most able players gravitate to their ranks. They are known to want a voice on the general committee, and it may be the case that at one stroke such a reform could heal the breach that exists between them and the ruling body. Perhaps the trimming of Schools representation on the WRU from two delegates to one would be a small price to pay for peace in the land. For their part the big clubs would accept in return a first-among-equals role, ceasing their noises off and adopting a collaborative position on major initiatives proposed by the WRU.

Certainly it is hard to see how the Union's declared aim of introducing leagues to Welsh Rugby can be achieved without the whole-hearted participation of the Merit Table group. Ironically, their glamour and crowd-appeal has made the Schweppes Cup competition an outstanding success; and yet they themselves have never had a direct say in its organisation. If they felt that their opinion was genuinely making itself felt, and co-operation rather than coercion was the WRU's aim, they might throw their weight behind the league proposals and assist the staging of what could be a valuable and progressive experiment.

New Zealand's World Cup captain David Kirk was outspoken at a Welsh Schools seminar in the autumn of 1988. Before an audience of schoolmasters he emphasised the importance of a successful National fifteen for the attraction of youngsters into the game. The skills and, in particular, the winning ways of All Blacks like Kirwan, Shelford and Whetton, he felt sure, were crucial factors in persuading Kiwis of a tender age to seek sporting fulfilment in Rugby football and thereby guarantee continuity of excellence in his country. Failure, or a suggestion that their heroes really had feet of clay, caused the young to turn away and identify with top performers in other fields, such as golfers or pop singers.

Certainly during the 'seventies it was the ambition of a host of schoolboys to be another Barry John or Mervyn Davies. Equally, the three recent thrashings at New Zealand's hands in successive summers, plus the losing streak of European results in 1988–89, must have damaged the belief of many in Welsh Rugby as a cause to embrace. No teenager wants to emulate players who are continually seen lining up behind their goal line, tails between their legs, waiting for conversion after conversion to sail over the bar.

The root cause of decline in Wales appears to many to lie in a discernible absence of basic skills. Dropped passes, missed tackles and inaccurate line kicking are common in the Welsh game at all levels. Centres who can make breaks – once the glory of three quarter play in Wales – are few and far between. Robert Norster's great ability to jump and catch is fundamental, yet he stands out almost alone as a line-out expert. Even John Ryan, who took over as National team coach in 1988, has been moved to express dismay and frustration at the arrival in his squad of players whose skills were not those he expected in would-be Test players – and were well below the level he had experienced when coaching his two Cup-winning sides of the 'seventies. Some doubt must hang over the efficacy of training sessions at schools and in the clubs: is too much time being spent on the scheming of 'moves' and ploys at the expense of basic chores which give an enduring foundation to a boy's capacity to play well?

There is also a dismal and depressing undercurrent of violence as opposed to aggression in the Welsh game, and the winter of 1988–89 witnessed some horrifying on-field thuggery. Many players do not seem to understand the difference between the legitimate use of the boot at rucks and the kind of stamping and raking which can cut an opponent's head open or batter him into unconsciousness. Vicious punches have been thrown – and it can only be hoped that miscreants have noticed that while their fists are flying vital tries are often being conceded. If only the energy released into such unarmed combat could be channelled into a constructive approach to match play.

The time is probably ripe for an examination in depth of the way in which Rugby values and skills are inculcated into the young. It is the stated view of leading clubs that schools, for instance, are not at present providing the opportunity, encouragement and quality coaching necessary to develop youngsters' skills. In the foreseeable future, however, the schools are bound to be the main and most important nursery of the game. This is where the WRU can take a helpful and constructive lead; if, for example, Rugby teachers are less keen to allot out-of-school time to tutoring and coaching pupils, then some of the enormous funds now pouring into the game should be allocated to reimburse these key men for extra-mural activities. Why not?

There could be help, too, in the form of visits to schools by the International and club stars of the day which the Union might encourage, perhaps by picking up receipts for lunch and petrol. Nothing quite stirs the imagination of twelve-year-olds like the genial presence of a celebrity in their school hall or gymnasium, or out on the Rugby pitch. Schoolmasters should not be slow to exploit such opportunities by capitalising on the willingness of many top players to talk to the young.

The vast majority of Welsh players are as conscientious as ever their predecessors were: concerned to achieve maximum fitness and improve their game as far as they possibly can. Match play with a good club remains the goal for most, with a cap for their country as an ambition to which the select few can aspire. Occasionally calls for broken-time payment surface, along with hints that fees should be paid for International appearances; but by and large player-power is not a major issue in Wales. If moves are made in the next decade in the direction of professionalism it is likely that the lead will come from the southern hemisphere, with the Welsh as reactors rather than trend-setters.

But coaching of the highest quality is needed, to harness and direct the enthusiasm and native ability of participants and to breed a disciplined approach. Actors need production; choirs need conductors; Rugby players, too, need the constant encouragement and assessment of an enlightened mentor.

Besides its problems, Welsh Rugby has a tremendous amount going for it in terms of tradition and experience. We turn now to the many assets possessed by the Principality in the shape of its great clubs and the multifarious venues where the game flourishes.

TAFF'S ACRE:

The 'Cardiff Arms' Park

On the afternoon of Saturday 4 February 1989 the national ground at Cardiff Arms Park presented a perennial sight. Stands and terraces were a tightly meshed kaleidoscope of red, green and white, as 50,000 Welshmen and 8000 Irish visitors cheered their favourites in the second round of the Five Nations Championship. Not a single unoccupied seat was to be seen; spectators on the west and east terraces stood shoulder to shoulder; and out in Westgate Street the usual empty-handed contingent without tickets cursed their luck before wandering off to seek consolation in front of a television screen. As the Honorary Treasurer of the Welsh Rugby Union had once declared to his committee when they contemplated the stadium's massive refurbishment, 'There will always be an excess of demand

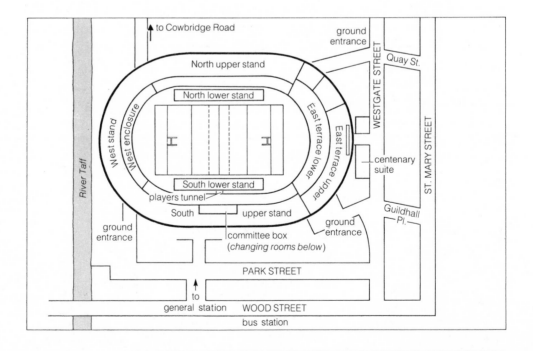

over the available accommodation for major International Rugby matches at Cardiff.'

Yet ironically, since the completion of the great national temple of Rugby some five years earlier, home supporters had been starved of success – and Ireland's victory by nineteen points to thirteen was Wales's sixth consecutive defeat at the hands of major opposition. After the all-conquering years a decade before, when New Zealand were the sole nation to win in Cardiff and only France (once) went home unbeaten, suddenly in their grand new premises the Welsh found success hard to achieve. Ireland's win was their third in three visits to Wales; France and Scotland won twice in the 'eighties; the 1984 Wallabies were overwhelming victors.

And yet the magic of Cardiff endures and the faithful still submit eagerly to its spell. Like all small nations, the Welsh crave victory almost to the point of desperation. But in their heart of hearts they know that, despite the result, it is ultimately the game that counts. And, in their case, the ground: more than any other Rugby arena in the world, Cardiff Arms Park has always been a theatre of the magnificent.

There are now, of course, two stadia, and the Welsh Rugby Union's next door neighbours are the senior occupants. Midway through the nineteenth century Isambard Kingdom Brunel straightened out a meander in the River Taff in order to bring his Great Western Railway through Cardiff and build a station on dry, well-drained soil. The tract of reclaimed land behind the Cardiff Arms coaching inn thus became available for recreation and, after dismissing plans for siting an open market there, its owner John, Third Marquess of Bute, made it over to local cricketers. In 1876 enthusiasts keen to play the new sport of Rugby football began using it in the winter months; Cardiff Rugby Football Club was born; and soon, as the game caught on like wildfire, the infant Welsh Football Union borrowed it for a representative match in which Ireland were the victims of Wales's first International victory.

For nearly a century this joint tenancy of the rapidly growing Rugby stadium continued, with club and county cricket flourishing close at hand. Cardiff RFC grew to be perhaps the best-known Rugby club in the world; the Welsh Rugby Union, though alternating home fixtures with St Helen's until 1954, based its administrative headquarters near the Park, and used the ground to stage matches against its four big European rivals as well as New Zealand, South Africa and Australia.

But a series of extremely wet winters in the late nineteen fifties and early 'sixties precipitated a crisis which had been simmering for many seasons. A succession of International matches took place on what can only be described as a quagmire, some of the greatest players in the world having their artistry reduced to pitiful dimensions and leaving the famous pitch with every orifice blocked by mud and slime. On one occasion the Irish were on the point of declining to take the field before 58,000 spectators – who would probably have run riot had they failed to appear.

Though the ground's infrastructure was in need of a complete overhaul, with rotting, rusting stand and terrace accommodation, the fundamental problem was over-use of the turf. Cardiff played first, second and youth team matches on it; there were county fixtures, schools matches and charity games; in addition the WRU required it for Trials and, since the rejection of Swansea as a suitable venue for representative football, up to three International games each winter. Always susceptible to flooding from the nearby Taff (and with its main drainage system irremediably damaged by German bombing during World War II), the pitch degenerated to a deplorable condition: in December and January it could resemble a paddy-field, while by April it might be as hard and unyielding to studs as a parade ground. In 1960, after the Springboks had won a 3–0 victory in a rainstorm, the Taff burst its banks and flooded the stadium to a depth of three feet.

It was then, prompted by Cardiff's city fathers, that the top administrators put their heads together and came up with the twin-stadia, £9 million concept that was to prove its salvation. The Welsh Rugby Union acquired the freehold of the ground, cricket moved up-river to Sophia Gardens, the Greyhound racing concern whose dogs had competed around the Rugby pitch's perimeter were bought out, and Cardiff RFC agreed to the laying-out of a smaller complex adjacent to the main ground. The grand plan was set in motion between 1968 and 1971 with the demolition and reconstruction of the present North Stand. There followed the integration of offices for the WRU and Cardiff RFC's reception rooms.

Now came a period when the Treasurer, Kenneth Harris, and his committee had to be brave. Progress needed to take place, yet the 'seventies brought with them a daunting period of galloping inflation which could make a nonsense of the most stringent budgeting. However, by converting the north terrace into a seated enclosure, cash was made available for funding the building of the west stand and, a year later, of the east terrace (which many would say is now the most colourful sector of the whole stadium on match days). By 1984 the U-shape had been completed with the reconstruction of the south stand at a cost of £4,500,000 – four times, be it noted, the cost of its twin north stand re-styled just a dozen years before. The mammoth work was over; and next door Cardiff RFC were well satisfied with their own ample playing provision inside a stadium holding some

17,000 spectators which had been opened back in 1970.

There were minor criticisms, about the ease of exit from grandstands and the control of the south terrace crowds, but for the most part there was satisfaction and praise from the Welsh Rugby public who knew that Cardiff Arms Park was now a complex to compare with any in the world. Expert ground managers like Bill Hardiman, Albert Francis and, later, Tony Horne saw to its maintenance and lavished care and attention on the pitches; and the WRU resolved that outstanding debts could be cleared by the end of the 'eighties.

But 1984 did not bring a real respite. The Welsh Rugby Union pressed on with refinements which improved the stadium and its facilities. The nub of the whole arena, which historically had been located beneath the north stand area, moved to the south side of the ground. Here palatial changing rooms were introduced beneath the grandstand's superstructure. Players preparing for a big game now have space to indulge their warming-up exercises. There are individual tubs, roomy plunge baths and batteries of showers. The toilets bear comparison with those in a five-star hotel. Special non-slip floors have been installed.

A couple of flights upstairs are reception rooms where the Union can entertain visiting VIPs. In the President's Room drinks can be served, followed by an excellent lunch, after which administrators can walk just a few paces to the south stand committee box where they sit directly above the half way line and the spacious deck set aside for television and radio crews. Other functions take place in the Centenary Suite below the east terrace, while Cardiff RFC have their own bars and lounges in the area between the two grounds.

Also beneath the south stand of the National Ground are to be found three training rooms with sand floors. Here players can use weights and practise line outs and scrummaging without damaging the turf outside. These premises are also used for lectures and for Press conferences after major games. There are also other rooms dotted around the great curve of the stadium where receptions, media briefings and private parties can take place. Somewhere, too, is the sound-proofed snug bar where the Big Five meet to choose their International XVs.

But the centrepiece of Cardiff Arms Park is its pitch. During the re-building period it was shifted some fifteen metres in a westerly direction, so that the legendary spot which all New Zealand visitors want to see – the red and black disc at the point where Bob Deans was denied his equalising try in 1905 – is now in the in-goal area beneath the east terrace. Soon after the south stand was completed, the absence of sunlight led to problems with the growth of grass in the south-west corner of the ground. At the same time Europe experienced a succession of harsh winters, when for five years in succession International matches had to be postponed because of frost or snow (not all of them at Cardiff). Thus in summer 1986 Kenneth Harris and the then WRU secretary Ray Williams paid fact-finding visits to Anfield and Goodison Park which led to the installation of a gas-fired undersoil heating system. This has eliminated the sense of panic experienced by groundsmen at the first hint of frost in January and February. The use of straw, elaborate plastic covering devices and even braziers is thus in the past; and the thermostatically controlled warmth radiating from the concealed pipes also has a beneficial effect upon the grass roots. This innovation, abetted by sand-slitting and new drains, has given Wales a playing surface for International rugby which is unsurpassed; New Zealand's great captain Graham Mourie once said, 'Oh, yes, we have pitches like this back home. But we use them for tennis and bowls.'

Another refinement in recent years has been the laying-down of an all-weather running track around the touchlines. The bends are too narrow for International athletics competition, but its lanes are ideal for Rugby players testing their speed and staying power. The Welsh squad makes use of it on training nights, as do local clubs and schools who book time with the WRU. Crack hurdlers Colin Jackson and Nigel Walker have limbered up on it, as have other members of Wales athletics coach Malcolm Arnold's elite cadre.

The completed Cardiff Arms Park, with its giant electronic information board, is a tremendous achievement: a superbowl of the amateur game. Conceived as a whole, it possesses a coherence which is lacked by the essentially impromptu improvements at Twickenham, Murrayfield and Lansdowne Road; and with its eastern end open to the sky it does not have the claustrophobic atmosphere of Parc des Princes (which is in any case a municipal stadium not owned by the French Rugby Federation).

And, pertinently, it is a gigantic money-spinner, the possible 'take' for the 1989–90 season amounting to a mind-boggling £2 million. The Jehovah's Witness organisation's summer rallies regularly feed largesse into the WRU's coffers, as do pop concerts given by entertainers like Michael Jackson, U2 and David Bowie.

But to be nouveau riche is to run into undreamed-of problems. One of the WRU's major preoccupations in the next decade will concern the redistribution of their huge new income: fairly, consistently, and to the greater good of the game.

However, everything in the garden should be lovely. Alone among the great

Rugby grounds of the world, Cardiff Arms Park stands at the very heart of a capital city, close to all its amenities. Ticket holders for the terrace, enclosure or grandstand, get a vivid view of the Rugby. Provision for players is unsurpassed.

Yet there are critics and those who have doubts whether, a quarter of a century ago, the WRU was right to put its eggs into the Cardiff basket.

The problem which exercises their minds is space. The main arena at Cardiff Arms Park is fashioned in a way which precludes further expansion. Should there be a renaissance of the Welsh game comparable to that which took place in the 'seventies, it would be impossible for the WRU to respond to spectator interest by contriving entry for, say, a further 10,000 spectators. The positioning of north, south and west stands is definitive, and there is no practicable way of increasing accommodation at the stadium's eastern end.

A second factor is crowd control, which became a genuine headache in the mid-'eighties, particularly on the south terrace. Calculations made when the Safety of Sports Grounds Act was passed in 1975 had assumed that a capacity crowd of 62,500 would assemble over a period of about two hours in traditional fashion. In practice it emerged instead that 30,000 spectators were choosing to arrive in the final thirty minutes before kick-off, creating an impossible situation for stewards and the police. Swaying, and the stretchering away of spectators overcome by the crush, became common sights. The WRU was soon given an ultimatum by the Welsh Office to reduce the capacity of Cardiff Arms Park by 6000. This led to the installation of seating on the south terrace in the summer of 1988, which cancelled out the problem in that area while leaving unsolved unsatisfactory aspects of the west and east terrace accommodation.

Difficulties have manifested themselves outside the ground too. It can only be approached from two sides, via Westgate Street (which the police now close to traffic on match days) or Park Street. It seems possible that before long a footbridge may have to be built across the Taff adjacent to Ground Entrance Six in order to ease the crush on pavements and roads outside. There is no doubt, in short, that the WRU feels itself to be constricted, and some senior members even hark back to the Bridgend solution which was an option back in the nineteen fifties.

However, there is little doubt that these problems are ones which the ruling body will have to live with for the foreseeable future. Nor are they considerations that weigh heavily with the 58,000 supporters who stand for the National Anthem at three o'clock on an International Saturday afternoon. For them, and for many lovers of the game elsewhere in the world, Cardiff Arms Park is still a mighty citadel whose capacity to generate legends and make men immortal outweighs arguments about comfort or convenience. 'Taff's Acre' is a field of praise.

Great International Days at Cardiff Arms Park

12.4.1884: Wales 2T 1DG, Ireland nil

In days before the awarding of points, this first home victory by Wales in International competition still appears to have been convincing. Seven Cardiff players were in the Welsh side, men who would have felt at home in the still spartan arena beside the River Taff. The 'Cardiff Arms' Park was then no more than an open enclosure, teams changing in a nearby hostelry, and it is likely that a crowd of no more than 5000 would have been in attendance.

The Irish arrived with only thirteen players, their number being made up by two Welshmen in H.M. Jordan and (probably) J. McDaniel. The Welsh try scorers were T. Norton and T.J.S. Clapp; W.H. Stadden dropped the goal.

7.1.1893: Wales 12pts, England 11pts

England, where the Rugby game originated, and Scotland with its network of public schools, had dominated the Championship's early years. Suddenly, however, with this notable first home win over their nearest neighbours, Wales were acknowledged as a power in the land, going on to beat Scotland and Ireland to take the title and a Triple Crown for the first time.

A.J. 'Monkey' Gould scored two captain's tries for his side, but became annoyed when Billy Bancroft chose to drop kick for goal when Wales were awarded a late penalty. Nonetheless the full back's aim was good and his kick won the game before 15,000 wildly enthusiastic spectators.

14.1.1905: Wales 25pts, England 0pts

This match, in the middle of Wales's first 'golden era', brought a seventh successive victory over England and the biggest losing margin experienced by the visitors until the 1972 side went down to France by 37–12. Wales ran in seven tries, including two by the wing Teddy Morgan.

16.12.1905: Wales 3pts, New Zealand 0pts

Teddy Morgan made sure of his place in Welsh Rugby's Valhalla with a clean-cut try scored at seven minutes to three o'clock which dropped the all-conquering First All Blacks to the only defeat of their tour. The visitors fell for a decoy run to their left by danger men Percy Bush, Gwyn Nicholls and Willie Llewellyn as scrum half Dicky Owen sent a reverse pass which Cliff Pritchard scooped up. Rhys Gabe received and sent Morgan a pass which just gave him room to out-pace opposition full back George Gillett on his way to the north terrace corner.

The excitement became almost unbearable for the 47,000 crowd as the All Blacks tried to save the day. Five minutes from time came the incident about which Welshmen and Kiwis have argued for over eight decades. Billy Wallace beat the defence and, a few yards from the goal-line, gave what would have been a scoring pass to centre Bob Deans who was cut down by a magnificent cover tackle by Teddy Morgan assisted by Gabe. The New Zealander attempted to wriggle his way across, only to be disallowed the try by referee John Dewar Dallas from Edinburgh.

There is no reason to imagine that Dallas, who had been capped as a back row forward by Scotland two years before, was not up with the play and well placed to see Deans's failure to release the ball after the tackle. His verdict was final, and Wales had scored perhaps the most memorable victory in their history. Now Cardiff Arms Park was truly on the world's Rugby map.

21.1.1922: Wales 28pts, England 6pts

The war was over; life was back to normal; and this victory and the Championship title which was to follow suggested that the Welsh could pick up the momentum that had lapsed in 1914. In fact it turned out to be a last defiant gesture from a nation that would plunge into the doldrums for a decade.

Played before a capacity crowd, the match was notable for the eight tries run in by the home side, Bowen, Delahay, Islwyn Evans, Hiddlestone, Parker, Palmer, Richards and Whitfield being the scorers. For spectators, recognition was made easier by the lettering worn by the players.

21.12.1935: Wales 13pts, New Zealand 12pts

The Welsh had taken a thrashing from the 1925 All Blacks at St Helen's, but now they took satisfying revenge in a match which kept 50,000 onlookers enthralled.

Their heroes were trailing 12–10 with some ten minutes left, and furthermore hooker Don Tarr had been stretchered from the field with a broken neck. Then Wilfred Wooller received from Cliff Jones and punted high to the All Blacks' line. He stretched his long legs to reach the bounce first, only for the ball to elude his grasp. Geoffrey Rees Jones, however, who had scored earlier along with Claude Davey, was at his heels and his dive made sure of the winning try.

25.3.1950: Wales 21pts, France 0pts

Wales's Triple Crown gained in Ireland a fortnight before this game was tarnished with tragedy, and before the kick off a minute's silence was observed by the capacity crowd in memory of the air crash victims who died on their way home from Dublin.

Then all was elation as the Welsh surged to a first Grand Slam since 1911. At this time the French were less organised and composed than they would be two decades later, and despite the presence of fine individuals like Jean Prat, Guy Basquet and Michel Pomathios they were no match for John Gwilliam's well-drilled side. Ken Jones (twice), Jack Matthews and Roy John were Wales's try-scorers, the remarkable Lewis Jones placing three conversions and a penalty goal.

19.12.1953: Wales 13pts, New Zealand 8pts

An extraordinary cross-kick by Clem Thomas helped clinch Wales's third victory over New Zealand. Cut off close to the south stand touchline, the Swansea flanker took possibly the only positive option open to him and punted high to the midfield at the Taff end of the ground. The bounce deceived Scott and Fitzpatrick, falling sweetly into the hands of Ken Jones, who had only to stroll beneath the All Blacks' crossbar for a try converted by Gwyn Rowlands. The wing had earlier converted a try by Sid Judd and placed a penalty goal.

Gareth Griffiths displayed tremendous courage on this day, being forced from the fray with a dislocated shoulder but returning to boost his fourteen team-mates for the final ten torrid minutes' resistance. Skipper Bleddyn Williams completed a remarkable double over New Zealand, having captained Cardiff to victory over the tourists a few weeks before.

29.3.1958: Wales 6pts, France 16pts

This was the day France came of age in world Rugby. Even the ranks of Tuscany could scarce forbear to cheer the stalwart effort which brought a first win at Cardiff and their highest score against Wales. Said Carwyn James afterwards, 'It was a bad day for Wales but a great day for Rugby football.' For once the French were a perfectly balanced side. The pack was powerful, and well led by the formidable Michel Celaya, while behind the scrum brilliant runners like Henri Rancoule, Roger Martine and Maurice Prat showed that Wales no longer had a monopoly of fast, clever three quarters. The Welsh were outscored by four tries to one.

15.4.1967: Wales 34pts, England 21pts

Defeated by Scotland, Ireland and France, Wales took the field against England as the underdogs with a Championship whitewash staring them in the face. David Watkins, however, proved a fine leader, opting for open play on the bone-hard April turf, and the uninhibited tactics he adopted proved decisive.

This was the 'Jarrett match', and the youngster's performance eclipsed feats which would have been notable on any other occasion: Gerald Davies has written mournfully how his own two tries, not a bad afternoon's work, were almost overlooked in the post-match euphoria; England's Roger Hosen's four penalty goals gave him his country's individual points record – 38 – for a Championship season. A lock, John Barton, scored two tries.

But Jarrett caught the eye as he relentlessly piled up 19 points, which equalled the Welsh record for an International game. His tally was made up of a try, five conversions and a penalty goal.

24.1.1970: Wales 6pts, South Africa 6pts

For the first time ever, Wales escaped defeat by the Springboks, a late Gareth Edwards try giving them parity. The scrum half also kicked a penalty goal, Sid Nomis and H.O. de Villiers having been South Africa's scorers. As usual the Springboks attracted a huge crowd, many of the onlookers being able to sit in the giant new north stand which had just been re-designed and re-built.

This, however, was South Africa's last appearance in Cardiff. Though lacking the All Blacks' charisma, their players had always been held in the very highest respect in Wales for their technical expertise and dour commitment. The growing clamour over their Government's racial policies, however, made it imprudent for another Rugby tour to Britain to be contemplated, especially in the light of the demonstrations and violence which accompanied the progress of Dawie de Villiers's men around the British Isles.

13.3.1971: Wales 23pts, Ireland 9pts

This was the third victory in Wales's magnificent Grand Slam of 1971, helping to inaugurate what was to be a golden decade. The Irish brought a strong, confident team to Cardiff Arms Park which stayed in the game well into the second half before falling victim to the new Welsh policy: subdue and penetrate.

The home team's splendid pack, with tight forwards Denzil Williams and Barry

Llewelyn at the height of their powers, first mastered a fiery Irish eight. Then in the second half the backs started finding their way to the line, a burst of fourteen points in sixteen minutes securing the victory. Gareth Edwards and Gerald Davies got two tries apiece, while the eleven-point contribution from the boot of Barry John demonstrated the precision which was to destroy New Zealand later that year.

27.1.1973: Barbarians 23pts, New Zealanders 11pts

This match, seen by 46,000 cheering fans, is chiefly remembered for the glorious opening try for the Baa-Baas, initiated by Phil Bennett close to the 22 and finished with a 30-metre burst by Gareth Edwards at the south-west corner flag. An opening salvo coming just three minutes into the match, it blasted open the All Blacks' defences.

What is less readily recalled is the overall quality of the rest of the game. Grant Batty's two tries for New Zealand, for instance, one scored after a deft chip over J.P.R. Williams's head, were models of superb wing play and helped to close the gap to 17–11 soon after the interval.

Ultimately it took another truly great try by the Barbarians, rounded off after a bout of handling lasting 90 seconds by John Williams, to put the result beyond doubt.

6.3.1976: Wales 19pts, France 13pts

This was the last match in which the great Mervyn Davies led Wales. Three weeks later he was stretchered from a cup-tie on the neighbouring club ground with an arachnoid haemorrhage of the brain which forced his retirement from the game.

Davies had been a thoughtful, meticulous captain of his country who also demonstrated his great courage in this game by staying to the bitter end despite being handicapped by a bruised thigh. It was fitting that he should go out of International football on a supreme note.

France presented the main challenge to Welsh supremacy during the 'seventies and this was one of a series of red-blooded encounters. The determination of the visitors meant that the Welsh had to be content with just a single try by J.J. Williams, the winning points coming from a series of penalty goals.

1.11.1980: Wales 3pts, New Zealand 23pts

This match revealed that for Wales the party was over. Her reshaped team had won their two home Championship games the previous winter, but now a magnificent All Black side led by Graham Mourie demonstrated that the new combination could not rank with their great predecessors of a couple of years earlier.

New Zealand scored four tries, the most memorable being Mourie's opening effort at the south-east corner and the killer blow administered in the second half by hooker Hika Reid after a long break by the midfield backs. Once a solo break by David Richards had been ruthlessly cut down on the half way line, the Welsh were never in the game.

After a decade blotted with controversy and a somewhat malign approach to the business of winning, New Zealand restored their high standing in Welsh eyes. This victory at Cardiff Arms Park, incidentally, was the last of a unique Grand Slam which had brought successive wins over Cardiff, Llanelli, Swansea and Newport.

20.3.1982: Wales 18pts, Scotland 34pts

If New Zealand had shown that Wales were now at the mercy of power Rugby from the southern hemisphere, Scotland's victory indicated that Cardiff Arms Park was no longer a forbidding proposition to the Europeans. On this occasion a combination of exuberant forward play and incisive running by the backs yielded the highest total ever scored against the Welsh in Wales.

Jim Calder got the first try after a thrilling 80-metre gallop upfield, Renwick, Pollock, White and Johnston following him to the line. Andy Irvine, who had often looked fallible in Cardiff, was in splendid form and his four conversions were supplemented by dropped goals from Renwick and Rutherford.

20.2.1988: Wales 25pts, Scotland 20pts

Although unable to produce consistently successful Rugby in the 'eighties, Wales still had men who could bring a crowd to its toes, and the striking power of Jonathan Davies and Ieuan Evans in this tremendous game of Rugby conjured up faint echoes of Welsh back play at its very best. Davies, in what was to be the last home Championship appearance of his fleeting career, pushed the ball along the ground after a scrum near Scotland's line and produced astonishing acceleration to outstrip the defence in a 15-metre burst to the line. Shortly afterwards it was a series of twinkling side-steps by Evans which brought an even more spectacular score.

Inspired by the big boot of Gavin Hastings and his four penalty goals Scotland fought their way back into contention, and it took two dropped goals by Davies to put them down. The 62,500 spectators went home knowing that, though the time had not yet returned when victory at Cardiff Arms Park could be anticipated with confidence, the stadium was still one whose ambience could inspire men to mighty deeds.

International Heroes of Cardiff Arms Park

All Welsh clubs have their heroes and demi-gods. Bars and reception rooms are festooned with the portraits and jerseys of the great players who have brought honour to their team, town and village. But above and beyond such parochial considerations there seems to me to be an identifiable group which belongs to the nation at large, men whose outstanding ability and dedication have endeared them to supporters everywhere and whose calibre has never been questioned. Their names, too, are the ones known and recognised far beyond Wales: they are the Superstars.

Erith Gwyn Nicholls was a West countryman who found fame in Wales, coming into the Cardiff side in 1893. He captained the club through four seasons, a jointly-held record, and played for Wales in three Triple Crown years, earning the title 'Prince of Threequarters'. He spent eighteen years in first-class Rugby and was the sole Welshman to tour Australia with the British side of 1899.

A contemporary wrote of him, 'He was an inspiring leader, a great handler of the ball who exploited gaps to create, unselfishly, tries for his colleagues.'

Ivor Jones, a Llanelli back row forward, won unreserved plaudits from that most critical of audiences, the New Zealanders, who rose to his exploits with the 1930 Lions. When he followed the 1969 Welsh tour as a spectator, Kiwis queued up to shake him by the hand.

Perhaps the most puzzling aspect of Jones's career was that after his return home he never again found favour with the Welsh selectors. Although his playing days stretched an impressive seventeen years from 1922 to 1939 he collected only fourteen caps.

Cruelly, the Second World War interrupted the career of many fine players, including **Wilfred Wooller**. Aged twenty-seven at the outbreak of hostilities, he exchanged Rugby kit for Army uniform, only to fall into the hands of the Japanese and return emaciated and weak to Wales in 1945. Undoubtedly he was at a peak in 1939, and although denied a chance to skipper Triple Crown or Grand Slam teams he remains one of the two or three outstanding all-round sportsmen in Welsh history.

Besides winning Rugby Blues, Wooller played cricket for Cambridge, captained Glamorgan and was elevated to England's Test cricket selection panel. After moving south from Llandudno, his eighteen-cap Rugby career was based at Cardiff where he developed into a clever and powerful centre.

Cliff Jones was Wooller's stand off half on numerous occasions for Cambridge University, Cardiff and Wales. First capped in 1934, he held the position throughout the decade, beating off a spirited challenge from Swansea's W.T.H. Davies. Jones, later a Welsh selector, is remembered for electric acceleration and a dazzling side-step. Critics with long memories name him as the best attacking stand off half of this century.

Though **Haydn Tanner** transferred to Cardiff after the war, he will forever be associated with Swansea, for whom he played in his formative years, and for his part in two wins over the 1935 All Blacks by his club and his country.

Many Welsh scrum halves have been diminutive, quicksilver figures on the field, but Tanner was a big man who turned the scales at fourteen stones. In his late 'teens and early twenties his main aim was to run and attack; but subsequently he learned to vary his game and keep opposing loose forwards guessing. Hence his breaks, when they came, frequently put him clear of defenders and led to tries.

'Austere' is the word used by those who played under him to describe **John Gwilliam** – and doubtless this quality stood him in good stead in later years as headmaster of Birkenhead School. An able line-out forward, he took Wales to two Grand Slams in 1950 and 1952, appearing as a lock and number eight forward. He also captained Wales on one of their bravest displays, the 6–3 defeat at the hands of the powerful 1951 Springboks.

Lewis Jones passed like a comet through the Rugby heavens, all too soon turning professional with Leeds for a £6000 fee.

He came into International football at the tender age of seventeen, and straightaway contributed to Wales's second win at Twickenham in 1950. A long diagonal break from full back (almost unheard of in those days) helped set up a try for Cliff Davies. Jones converted it and kicked a penalty. Besides incisive running with a deceptively lazy stride, he could place-kick accurately from exceedingly long range.

Bleddyn Williams was certainly the finest centre in Britain in the post-war era. A beautifully balanced runner, his breaks were often made with the celebrated 'jink' – a side-step carried out without loss of pace. Williams was also a superb timer of passes, to which the tries scored by his wings bear witness.

He made 283 appearances for Cardiff between 1945 and 1955, winning twenty-two caps and touring New Zealand with the Lions in 1950. His finest hours came in 1953 when he skippered club and country to victories over the All Blacks.

Some of Wales's most important tries between 1947 and 1957 were scored by Newport's **Ken Jones**, who grafted considerable Rugby skills onto his shattering speed as a sprinter. The latter brought him Olympic fame at Wembley in 1948 and he wore a Welsh vest on the track at the 1954 Empire Games.

Jones won the first of his forty-four caps (for some time a record) against England at Cardiff in 1947. But perhaps his best match came at Twickenham in 1952 when his clever support of breaks by Cliff Morgan brought two sensational tries which helped set his country on course for a Grand Slam. Another of his seventeen International tries was the winning score against New Zealand in 1953.

On that occasion, Jones ran onto an inspired cross kick by **Clem Thomas** (Cambridge University and Swansea), who thus earned his own place among Wales's immortals. Thomas was a fine back row forward, feared by stand off halves for his speed around the pitch and for his uncompromising tackling. In retirement he has been a perceptive and outspoken Press and television critic.

For many seasons the most charismatic figure in Welsh rugby was the ebullient Rhondda-born **Cliff Morgan**. After a painfully learned tactical lesson on his third International appearance against South Africa in 1951, when his kicking played into the hands of the Springbok cover, Morgan emerged in 1952 as a dynamic stand off half capable of cutting a defence to shreds.

His years of glory began at Twickenham in 1952 when he masterminded the Welsh back play which conquered England and swept his country to a Grand Slam. Next year he was demoralising the Fourth All Blacks with Cardiff and Wales, and he reached a summit of achievement in the Test series of 1955 which the British Isles shared with South Africa.

Onllwyn Brace, something of a nomad among scrum halves (his clubs included Oxford University, the RAF, Aberavon, Llanelli and Newport), belongs in Wales's roll of honour for the tactical innovation and breadth of vision which enabled him to see a huge variety of options from just behind the pack. He is certainly one of Rugby football's great thinkers.

Brace could never quite import his concept of Rugby from Oxford into the conservative Welsh scene and won only nine caps. But in his playing days, and later as a television producer, he was able to open men's eyes to the game's wider possibilities.

Only two caps came the way of **Carwyn James**, against Australia (when he dropped a goal) and against France. It was his ill luck to be a contemporary and rival of Cliff Morgan.

He is, however, remembered as the outstanding British coach of the twentieth century. James perfected his skills in man-management within the peaceful cloisters of Llandovery College, from where he emerged to tutor Llanelli RFC (and coach a West Wales XV which gave the 1967 All Blacks a fearful run for their money). His big challenge came in 1971, when he was appointed coach to the Lions in Australasia. James rose to it magnificently, and the rest is history. He proved that the 2–1 Test series victory, with one match drawn, was no fluke when he coached his club to their famous win over Ian Kirkpatrick's All Blacks.

Clive Rowlands is a larger-than-life character who has operated successfully in various capacities through three decades of Welsh rugby history. He was a dogged scrum half who kicked too often for many people's liking ('Kick me the salt, dad,' his children were alleged to say at mealtimes). But his tactics were often right for the occasion, and he led Wales to a Triple Crown in 1965 (and was mysteriously ignored by the Big Five ever after). Later he coached the National XV, was a selector, and was appointed manager of the British Isles side to Australia in 1989.

The finest Newport stand off half of this century was **David Watkins**. A diminutive but sturdy player he won all the honours Rugby Union could offer before joining Salford RL club as a professional in 1967.

For much of the 'sixties Watkins was a prime crowd-puller at Rodney Parade and elsewhere. People flocked to marvel at his speed off the mark, side-steps with either foot and sustained pace that could hold off pursuit. Sometimes he ran too far, or became trapped through trying to beat one defender too many – in which case he would utilise an effortless kicking technique to extract himself and his team from trouble.

Unlike many other League captures, Watkins parted company from the Union game on the best of terms. Consequently, having resettled in the south, he remains a valued member of the Rugby fraternity.

John Dawes, currently Coaching Organiser to the Welsh Rugby Union, was a gifted centre with deep tactical insight. A product of Lewis School, Pengam, and UCW Aberystwyth, he captained London Welsh during their great years in the late 'sixties and used the club as his springboard into the Welsh team. His elevation to the captaincy of the British Lions in 1971 took many by surprise, but he emerged as a fine leader who could command a Test place in the centre on merit. After winning the series Dawes rubbed salt into the All Blacks' wounds by captaining the successful Barbarians side against them in 1973.

The name of **Keith Jarrett** belongs in this number, not because its bearer was among the very front rank of Welsh International players but because he is a living legend.

It was Jarrett who, as an eighteen-year-old in 1967, blazed a glorious nineteen points to beat England almost off his own bat. He capped an unforgettable 60-metre sprint for a try at the north-east corner of Cardiff Arms Park with five conversions and two penalty goals. In many people's opinion that display, and that match, re-fuelled Welsh rugby idealism and heralded the great decade of the 'seventies.

Gareth Edwards played himself quietly into International rugby football in the same year, taking advice from all who would offer it and perfecting the pulsating service which completed his all-round ability as a player. He showed his strike power against England at Twickenham with the first of twenty International tries, but for some seasons remained in the shadow of his first half back partner Barry John.

But by the summer of 1974, when John had been succeeded by Phil Bennett, Edwards was at a peak. South Africa had no answer to his immense strength and raking tactical kicks. He returned to Wales to play four more Championship seasons, and is acknowledged to be the finest scrum half to have represented his country. Edwards signed off in 1978 with a dropped goal in Wales's Grand Slam clincher against France.

In 1971 **Barry John** was King. He had demonstrated his ability and courage through the 1971 Grand Slam season, scoring a classic cat-burglar's try at Colombes in the process. Now he went to New Zealand, where his cool approach was central to the defeat of the All Blacks by the Lions. His precise kicking, with either foot, completely upset the New Zealanders' game-plan and was the direct reason for the dropping of their feared full back Fergie McCormick.

John could side-step, swerve, accelerate, handle, place kick and drop goals. He could ghost through defences like a wraith and, though slender of frame, make and withstand strong tackles. He was a very complete player indeed.

John – J.P.R. – Williams is widely accepted as the outstanding full back of the second half of the twentieth century. Many people's enduring memory of him is surging into the three quarter line and sometimes smashing his way through to the goal-line for a vital try (he scored six for Wales). But he was also a brave tackler, a last line of defence which withstood most assaults.

Williams came into the Welsh side as a nineteen-year-old at Murrayfield in 1969 and, though injuries interrupted his career once or twice, was a fixture until 1981 by which time he had been honoured with the captaincy of his country. A useful place kicker, he was also a crack tennis player.

It is hard to imagine a more exciting player than **Gerald Davies**. This product of Queen Elizabeth Grammar School, Carmarthen, who played for Cambridge University, London Welsh, Cardiff, the Barbarians, Wales and the British Isles, was a devastating runner with a superb side-step which he carried out without loss of pace. A sure handler of the ball, he scored twenty tries for Wales, a record which he shares with Gareth Edwards.

As skipper of Cardiff, Davies is remembered for a magnificent cup display at Pontypool where his outgunned forwards got just enough ball for him to win the day with four superlative tries.

In front of such great backs Wales were lucky enough to be able to call on forwards of equal calibre; and among them **Mervyn Davies** ranks as a giant. The Rugby world was saddened when a brain haemorrhage ended his career at twenty-nine.

'Swerve' – a sardonic nickname for a rather ungainly guy – was one of Rugby's winners. He was in three Triple Crown and two Grand Slam sides. With the Lions in New Zealand he denied New Zealand vital line out ball. In 1974, having switched clubs from London Welsh to Swansea, he was with the Lions again, this time helping in the defeat of South Africa.

Agile as a jumper, muscular at mauls, tireless as a covering defender, Davies made thirty-eight appearances for Wales. On the field his trademarks were a bristling bandit moustache and the broad swathe of white bandage which protected his ears.

Born at Watford of Welsh parentage, **John Taylor** was another of 'Harry Bowcott boys' from Old Deer Park, who like Mervyn Davies owed his first break to the then London-based selectors' percipience. This skilled and thoughtful flanker experienced a disconcerting start to his International career, finding himself in losing Welsh fifteens in six of his first seven outings. His country persevered with him, however, and he went on to become one of the most constructive forwards of his era. He toured twice with the British Isles and was a member of the highly successful Welsh sides of 1969 and 1971. In the latter year he earned immortality with a late, nail-biting conversion at Murrayfield which helped Wales to a one-point win and an eventual Grand slam.

In Barry John, **Phil Bennett** had a hard act to follow. After a demanding tour of South Africa in 1974 the little man from Llanelli suffered a reaction and lost his Wales team place to John Bevan. Once back in the saddle, however, he served his country well for three more seasons on the end of the big Edwards pass and captained the Lions in New Zealand in 1977, nearly managing to draw the Test series.

Bennett was a brilliant runner from broken play, and kicked accurately off the ground and from the hand. Television appearances in recent years show how deeply he thinks about the game.

Graham Price astonished the Rugby world when, at Parc des Princes on his debut in 1975, he scored Wales's final try after a 70-metre sprint. The feat demonstrated one of this fine prop's greatest attributes, superb fitness.

Strong, clever and unyielding, Price was a superb forward who served Wales loyally until 1983. With forty-one appearances he is his country's most capped forward.

Because success has come more rarely in the 'eighties, it has been hard for the modern generation to command an unassailable place in the esteem and affections of Welsh supporters. Probably the only superstar to emerge has been **Jonathan Davies**, who turned professional with Widnes for a record sum in January 1989.

Because he found himself behind packs who were usually unable to dominate their opponents, Davies seldom had the licence enjoyed by predecessors like John and Bennett. It is to his eternal credit that he created opportunities to register match-winning tries, often the result of his shattering speed of thought and foot. He could kick well, subject to occasional lapses of concentration, and dropped important International goals. I have to add that, of all the stand off halves I have watched, Davies is the one who most often managed to make the field around him seem briefly devoid of defenders.

The Welsh roll of honour is long and glorious, and those men who appear in it are special in global rugby terms. At the present time names are being added only sporadically; but what is certain, given the fertile seed-bed that is Welsh Rugby, its players and its clubs, is that the list will grow and glitter just as brightly in the decades – and the century – that lie ahead.

THE
GREAT CLUBS

ABERAVON RFC

HQ: The Talbot Athletic Ground
Strip: Red and black hoops

Climb to the hill-top above Margam Abbey and look south-west past the trees whose trunks and branches cower before the fierce prevailing wind. Gaze over the prospect below, one that encompasses old and newer aspects of industrial south Wales.

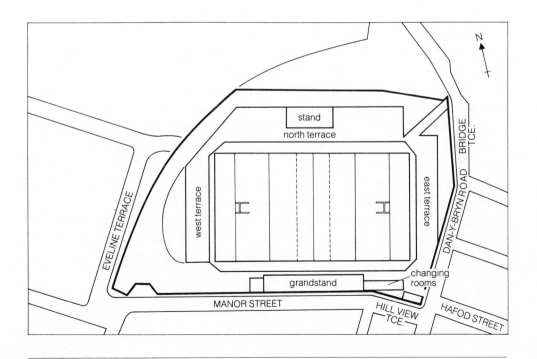

Far away, Swansea Bay curls around to Mumbles Head. The middle distance is dominated by the smoking, steaming profile of the great steelworks which for decades has breathed life and vitality into Port Talbot's economy with, away to the right, the sleek new factories that are relegating smokestack industry to history. Nearer still sprawls the slate roof patchwork that is the bulk of Port Talbot's housing stock. And in the immediate foreground, tucked close beside the M4 on its urban viaduct, can be seen the green rectangle of the Talbot Athletic Ground, its floodlight towers at each corner.

Not a vista to inspire, certainly, but one to fascinate – and to strike some as a 'Euclidian nightmare'. That was the late Richard Burton's description of its higgledy piggledy streets and crescents and closes. And Aberavon was Burton's club, its players his childhood heroes. Not that he ever paid to watch them play. As a boy he reached the ground via the railway line, Duffryn yards, and the siding behind the popular bank; as an adult he was always a VIP, the honoured guest of the club. In company the revered names tripped off his tongue: Ned Jenkins, Miah McGrath, the dreaded Bascombe brothers – 'God created Rugby to save the Bascombes from the gallows' – and later Ashton, Brace, O'Connor. To Aberavon, and to its Rugby team, Burton pledged his continuing allegiance. 'Until death,' as he once wrote.

Of all Wales's big clubs, Aberavon seem the best integrated into the surrounding community, above which their premises jut in the manner of an old-established inner-city soccer stadium such as Anfield in Liverpool. The Athletic ground was laid and fenced off by a local firm run by an immigrant Scot called Andrew Scott (whose son in later times contributed substantially to the re-development of Cardiff Arms Park, in particular the North Stand). From the start the turf's quality must have been excellent, since it was commandeered as a 'dig for victory' allotment during World War I. By a curious coincidence the Government also found it a role between 1939 and 1945, this time as a site for the barrage balloons which protected Port Talbot's docks and factories.

On three sides of the perimeter run terraces of snug villas in whose gardens spotless lines of week-end washing are often to be seen flapping in the breeze on match days. Guests and visitors step straight off the street into hospitable bars and reception rooms below a grandstand whose seating provision is ample, if spartan, and which dates back to 1921. The banked-up surrounds, partially covered with a canopy on the north side, were re-furbished with concrete steps in a £61,000 Government-assisted scheme at the outset of the 'eighties. Teams change in a light, modern extension to the stand which also houses a small gymnasium and medical room. The Aberavon welcome in recent years has been warm and smiling, with club President Lord Heycock – 'Llew' to his friends – and stalwarts like Gwilym Treharne and Hywel Thomas to the fore.

Despite such comforts, however, an undercurrent of unease has troubled Aberavon for some seasons. Leading players like Raymond Giles, Jeff Jenkins, Ian Brown, Billy James and David Joseph have turned their backs on the club to seek fulfilment elsewhere. Coaches and assistant coaches have arrived, and departed. Worse, the record of sendings off has been unenviable, culprits in the last decade having included two club captains in Allan Martin and Adrian Owen. The trend touched rock bottom in 1987–88 when five players were dispatched to early baths. As a result the club were suspended by the Welsh Rugby Union for two weeks at the outset of the new season and barred from match play until mid September.

Aberavon's first 'team manager', John Richardson, resigned in the summer of 1988 after less than twelve months in command. His successor Neville Walsh, a local solicitor, faced an uphill battle to unite the club, quell internecine disputes and quarrels, and recreate in the players' ranks a sense of loyalty and purpose. A breezy extrovert, Walsh was quick to deduce that man-management was the key to bringing calm – plus some of the old Wizardry – back to the Talbot Athletic Ground.

His stewardship received a major setback in the autumn of 1988 when, for the first time in seventeen years' competition in the Schweppes Cup, Aberavon were dismissed by a junior club – none other than their near neighbours Aberavon Quins. The 'Wizards' full recovery threatens to be long and agonising – and it will have to take place without Walsh, who resigned in April 1989.

And why do the club bear this nick-name? It derives from their unsurpassed record in the early decades of the century. In 1914 they were the last winners of the old South Wales Challenge Cup, discontinued after the War because the exchanges had become too violent. Ten years later they took the unofficial clubs' Championship, a feat that the Evening Post saluted with the headline 'Wizards of the West'. It was dreamed up by journalist W.H. Taylor, 'Rover' to his readers.

Since those times, despite maintaining a respectable playing standard, the club has rarely made winning headlines. The Championship title of 1961 was an exception. Under Rory O'Connor's captaincy, skill and teamwork were grafted onto the basic robustness of a side full of steelworkers to yield forty wins out of forty-eight matches, with just four defeats.

There were near misses, too, in 1974 and 1975 when the Wizards lost successive Cup Finals to Llanelli.

2.5.1914: Aberavon 10pts, Blaina 0pts

Aberavon's early teams contained a leavening of representatives who worked at the Port Talbot steelworks. Perhaps they included more brawn than brain. Certainly the Western Mail once observed, 'they can always produce a host of good forwards but fail to provide any decent three quarters.'

However, by 1914 the balance had been put right and Aberavon closed the first chapter in their history with a memorable win over Blaina in the Welsh Challenge Cup Final. Played at Bridgend before a big crowd, the match proved the climax to a string of fine victories. Fred Potter, an outside half who later joined Cardiff, was man of the match, scoring and converting two tries.

2.3.1946: Aberavon 4pts, Kiwis 17pts

Beginning in 1908, when they lost to the First Wallabies 0–15, Aberavon's meetings with major touring sides have usually been in uneasy unison with their old rivals Neath. Some would say that half a loaf has been better than no bread; others would maintain that disagreements over team selection, key positions and even the kit to be worn, plus a procession of indifferent results, are evidence of an experiment that has regularly failed.

Not that the Wizards have exactly excelled when playing under their own colours. But at least undiluted club pride has been given an airing, as when the Kiwis came to the Talbot Athletic Ground for the last match of their unforgettable post-war tour. After a rare reverse against Monmouthshire a few days earlier, the tourists badly wanted to go out in a blaze of glory with a big score, but brave Aberavon fought them tenaciously despite being reduced at one stage to thirteen men through injuries.

The home team were trailing 11–0 and out of contention by the break, after which Len Howard salvaged some pride with a dropped goal. But the 18,000 spectators took home with them magical memories of the great Bob Scott, probably the pick of New Zealand's attacking full backs. He contributed a conversion and penalty goal, besides setting up the finest of the tourists' four tries which Jim Kearney finished off after half a dozen team-mates had handled.

27.4.1974: Aberavon 10pts, Llanelli 12pts
26.4.1975: Aberavon 6pts, Llanelli 15pts

In the mid 'seventies, their last sustained period of supremacy, the Wizards came tantalisingly close to lifting major trophies. They went into the 1974 Cup Final as slight favourites – not only because Llanelli had left out their four British Lions-elect but also as a result of their win at Stradey Park a month earlier. A live-wire opening by their pack brought rucked possession on the Scarlets' goal-line and a chance for John Bevan to slip Steve Roper in at the corner. Flattering to deceive, alas, Aberavon slowly succumbed to a superhuman effort by Llanelli's below-strength team and four penalties from Andy Hill.

Twelve months later defeat was even more melancholy. For several months of the season Morton Howells's side led the Championship, only to be overtaken by Pontypool at the finish. Then, in the Cup Final, it was their turn to be without key players, Ian Hall and John Bevan having been hurt while representing Wales. Phil Bennett was in his most devastating form for Llanelli, setting up three decisive tries to which two penalties were the only reply. Runner-up status was Aberavon's yet again.

22.2.1986: Llanelli 10pts, Aberavon 11pts

The 1985–86 season saw Aberavon extract a measure of revenge from Llanelli after their two Cup Final reverses of a decade earlier, beating them twice in Championship fixtures and knocking them out of the Cup.

At this juncture in their history the Wizards looked full of promise. Former flank forward Richie Davies had taken over from Clive Shell as coach; Richard Diplock, Tim Fauvel and Ian Brown were promising newcomers, and the busy little stand off half Mike Lewis had returned from a sojourn in Italy. Nevertheless their Fourth Round visit to Stradey Park, where only one other club had ever won a Cup tie, was a chilling prospect.

Despite unflinching resistance by an Aberavon pack in which Fauvel and Brown were outstanding, the Cupholders led 10–7 until the stroke of time. Then scrum half Raymond Giles caught the Scarlets napping with a blind side dash which went on and on unchecked and finished with a dive to the corner flap for a marvellous try which brought an unforgettable victory.

But Aberavon were running out of steam. The semi-final brought defeat by Newport, and the onset of the Troubles, which were to prove chronic.

Aberavon's Heroes

Somerset-born policeman **Alfred ('Bobby') Brice** came to Aberavon on a posting to Taibach at the turn of the century. He was to win eighteen Welsh caps between 1899 and 1904 as a tearaway back row forward, taking part in two Triple Crown campaigns.

His International career came to an abrupt end. As Wales trooped off the Belfast pitch in 1904, having lost 12–14 to Ireland, he called referee Crawford Findlay a 'thundering idiot'. The penalty was an eight-month suspension – and no further caps.

Only a few weeks before the Belfast incident he had scored a magnificent try for Wales against Scotland at Swansea, smashing his way across the line through a cluster of defenders.

To pile up twenty-one caps in the inter-war era, in the days before tours and World Cups became regular occurrences, was a great feat, especially for a forward. That is why the name of **E.M. 'Ned' Jenkins** ranks high on Aberavon's roll of honour.

Contemporary reports make him sound uncannily like a modern New Zealand tight forward, able to hold his own with the backs at sprint practice but, at seventeen stones in weight, a tremendous provider of possession from the line outs and mauls. Another policeman, Jenkins was also a formidable athlete who, after retirement from Rugby in 1936, became Welsh shot-putt and discus champion.

The five McGraths noted in Rugby Football's annals as having won caps all played for Ireland. None of them could have been a greater character than **Miah McGrath**, who never played for Wales – or Ireland – but is revered as one of Aberavon's immortals.

In the 'thirties he captained the club for two seasons, and was in the combined Neath-Aberavon team which gave Benny Osler's Springboks a cracking game before going down 8–3. Decades later he was still father-confessor and guru-in-general, helping in the changing rooms, accompanying away teams, offering technical advice to anyone who would listen – and, if young players had had too heavy a night on tour, putting them to bed.

*

In the early 'sixties Aberavon boasted a number of tough young front row forwards of whom the most formidable was undoubtedly **Len Cunningham**. With hair close-cropped, this was a veritable pocket battleship of a prop with an unmistakable physical presence. He made fourteen appearances for Wales, including a Test against South Africa on the 1964 tour.

Cunningham was a cornerstone of the pack in his club's Championship season of 1961. Skipper Rory O'Connor, Phil Morgan, Cliff Ashton, Kelvin Coslett and jovial John Collins were other stars of the Wizards' finest post-war season.

John Bevan, who died in 1986 at just 38, can lay just claim to being the best all-round back in his club's history. The records show only four caps against his name for, unfortunately, the career of this gifted Neath Grammar School product was interrupted by injury at crucial junctures, allowing his great rival Phil Bennett to nose ahead of him in the International stakes.

Bevan made a sensational debut in the 25–10 victory of 1975 at Parc des Princes, the best by Wales in the French capital for 65 years. His backs were released straight and true, tearing great holes in the French defence. A victory over England followed, but before half-time in the match against Scotland, Bevan made a dejected exit holding an arm that hung limply from an injured shoulder. He played only once more for Wales, but was clearly admired by coach John Dawes who took him as the second stand off half behind Bennett on the 1977 Lions' tour.

The Bevan-Bennett argument raged fiercely between supporters for several seasons. Aberavon's man did not have the devastating ability of his rival to rip apart a defensive screen from broken play; but he was undeniably bolder than Bennett at drawing tacklers onto him so as to create space for team-mates.

His last service to Welsh Rugby before his tragically early death was to coach the National XV between 1982 and 1985.

The Lions called **Allan Jeffrey Martin** 'Panther' for his unobtrusive social skills. But his expertise in match-play was eye-catching, superb line-out work in particular helping to earn him thirty-four caps, for long the most by any Welsh lock forward.

After early years as a pupil at Sandfields, Martin moved to the great finishing school of Welsh Rugby, Cardiff Training College, later re-christened the South Glamorgan Institute of Higher Education. He came into the Welsh side as a mid-line jumper in 1973 against Australia, remaining his country's first choice in the position for eight years – Swansea's Geoff Wheel was his partner on twenty-eight occasions.

Martin was a reliable and powerful goal-kicker, who set an Aberavon points record of 285 points in 1974 which stood for nine years before falling to Mike Lewis. 'Panther' also placed important goals for Wales.

Raymond Giles moved to Cardiff late in his career after internal disagreements about Aberavon's tactical priorities. Born at Pyle, he succeeded the versatile Clive Shell in the Wizards' ranks and was a tremendous clubman. And just as poor Shell played through the Gareth Edwards era, so it was Giles's bad luck to be a contemporary of the redoubtable Terry Holmes, a factor that confined his International appearances to just two.

One of Giles's most memorable honours was captaincy of the 1980 Welsh Youth tour to South Africa, where the Test was won.

The Welsh Youth hooker against France at Pontypool Park in 1976 wore hair down to his shoulder blades. It was the fashion in those days – but there were still die-hards who groaned and wondered what the world was coming to.

Fifteen years later, with a truly distinguished career behind him, **Billy James** has silenced all the doubters. During most of Aberavon's troubles and tribulations in the 1980s, his loyalty never wavered. He could have quickly washed his hands of dissension and hassle. He could have promptly followed the example of many contemporaries and gone off to another club – where indeed he might have tasted victory more regularly and maybe found other forwards more ready to share the hard graft up front. But he stayed on; and must have had his patience stretched beyond the limit when he finally moved to Swansea at the outset of the 1988–89 season – a decision on which he has refrained from commenting. Despite this late change of allegiance, James is bound to go down as one of the Wizards' great men.

Wales awarded him more than a score of caps between 1983 and 1987, thereby acknowledging his consummate skill in the close exchanges, and his International career climaxed in 1987 with the captaincy of his country. Thereafter his dwindling mobility prevented him from holding off youthful rivals.

BRIDGEND RFC

HQ: The Brewery Field
Strip: Blue and white hoops

There are no manuals for television commentators. In September 1970 I turned up at the Brewery Field, Bridgend, to undertake my first televised Rugby football assignment for BBC Wales with little more than a good deal of enthusiasm and some preparation based on an article I had read about the great radio broadcaster

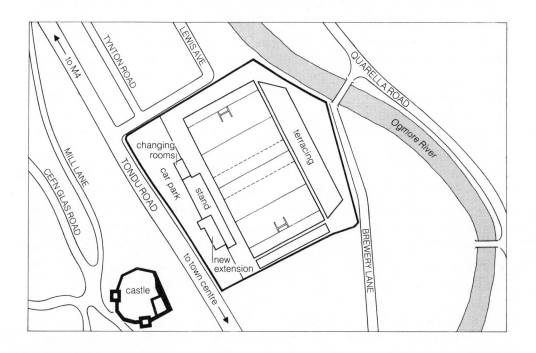

Raymond Glendenning. His homework for covering a major soccer match, it seemed, included the use of special cards coloured like the shirts of the two clubs involved. As his wife flipped them face up before him, Glendenning snapped out the name of the player who was to wear the number revealed. This was the secret of his instant identification, said the article, pointing out that the speed of football action left no time for commentators to glance down at their programmes to check players' names. I prepared for Bridgend's match against Newbridge accordingly.

Alas for my expectations. Rugby football, especially its forward exchanges, is often a confused affair compared with soccer's simple clarity. For much of the time players run towards or across the eye-line and finish up on their backs with numbers obscured – with the result that much of my preparation for that day was negatived. To compound my dilemma, as the television roller-coaster swung inexorably on its way, there was a kaleidoscope of names to get the tongue around. Newbridge had two if not three members of the Shipp family on board whose Christian names had to be unscrambled. Bridgend had Lyndon Thomas, Leighton Thomas and Lyn Davies to get right, plus a variety of Williamses and Joneses. It was a hard lesson for a beginner, but also the start of enlightenment and regular visits to training nights and changing rooms to ascribe the right names to the right faces.

I imagine that Newbridge and Bridgend have forgiven me for those early stammerings. Certainly, in the case of the latter, my welcome at the trim clubhouse beside the road which leads out of the town towards Maesteg has never been less than warm. And had I known it, I was fortunate in beginning to take a professional interest in the mid Glamorgan side at the outset of the greatest period in their history.

Bridgend RFC were scarcely an overnight sensation. Founded in 1878 they spent three-quarters of a century ambling along in the middle ranks of Welsh Rugby. Probably what shocked them out of complacency was the loss of the Brewery Field to the professional code in 1948–49 when a newly-formed Rugby League side secured the lease and amateur Rugby was banished for a decade to the Bandstand Field with its primitive facilities. During this time the tolerance and understanding of opponents like Cardiff, Newport and Llanelli was considerable and Bridgend have never forgotten the debt they owe to clubs who kept faith with them.

The local Council's purchase of the ground in 1957 and the grant of a lease provided the club with a springboard to glory from which they speedily leaped.

Until 1964 their honours board had lacked major distinctions. Then, suddenly, the years of achievement were at hand; and after two seasons as runners-up, Bridgend became unofficial Welsh club champions, a feat they repeated in 1966, 1970, 1971 and 1981. They became one of the country's leading seven-a-side practitioners, and crowned the seasons of success with four consecutive appearances in the Schweppes Cup Final from 1979 to 1982, winning the trophy twice. They supplied a string of able players to Welsh and British Isles representative sides.

Support burgeoned and the Brewery Field acquired the accoutrements of a major Rugby centre. Bridgend's first move after the Council gave them security of tenure for ninety-nine years was to re-furbish the changing rooms, after which they turned their attention to spectator comforts. There followed the erection of the 'cowshed', which turned the town-end terrace into a covered enclosure. Concrete steps were run along the popular bank, and the grandstand underwent successive extensions which gradually lifted its capacity to 1600 seats (some four hundred of which are today reserved for the club's special category of 'patrons'). Bars and kitchens were fitted out beneath the stand, while on the first floor there are now spacious lounges which can accommodate a throng of members and their guests on match days. A startling £200,000 has just been spent on a magnificent long room running behind the grandstand with windows looking out over the pitch. Nowadays the Brewery Field can hold 16,000 fans for a big Cup tie or tour game, while the television and radio deck slung beneath the stand has afforded media coverage worthy of the attractive Rugby played there.

Undoubtedly one factor behind the club's rise and rise has been the transformation of Bridgend from a medium-sized market town to a major industrial centre where many of the world's great manufacturing companies have located. The Ford Motor Company have embarked upon a multi-million-pound expansion at their engine plant, the biggest single investment ever made in Britain's motor industry. The Japanese firm Sony make TV sets at their Waterton Cross base, their presence underlined by the trim scoreboard which they erected above the Brewery Field's popular bank. And native Welsh businessmen have been equally generous: Bernard Davies, chief of a Bryncethin-based builders' merchants business, furnished one of the new reception lounges at a personal cost thought to be in excess of £20,000.

Such eagerness to invest and improve is consistent with the willingness to innovate which Bridgend have shown in the last three decades. The single most important step they took – and one which has had a profound influence on their style of play – was the appointment in 1964 of Cadfan Davies as club coach. This was the first post of its kind in British Rugby, demonstrating the club's readiness to take on board the new ideas being promulgated at WRU headquarters to lift the Welsh game out of the trough into which it had fallen.

Davies took control of a team which at the time had little physical stature or presence. He compensated for his men's lack of height and weight with a novel philosophy which set great store by skill and speed. He has written, 'Our aim was simple: to play continuous Rugby involving fifteen players; to run the opposition off their feet; to be at break-downs before rucks could be set up; to retain possession; and to attack opponents at all times, particularly when they were at their most vulnerable – in our twenty-five.' A quarter of a century on, this is still good Rugby thinking.

If they were trend-setters with regard to coaching, however, Bridgend have shown a reluctance curious in so forward-looking a club to ride the other great groundswell of recent years and favour the introduction of leagues. They have accepted Merit Table competition enthusiastically, and when the first *Rugby World* seventy-club 'Super-league' was published in 1981 took great delight in trumpeting their position at the top. Up to now, however, they have rejected the WRU league initiative: 'no-one should dictate to a club who it should play, where it should play and when it should play.' This, however, is exactly the principle governing the Schweppes Cup competition, in which they have enjoyed great success. Given their attitudes and character, it might be expected that the anti-league stance will be modified early in the 'nineties.

During their three great decades of progress Bridgend RFC have been fortunate in the quality of their administrators. Dr Peter Williams has functioned as an impressive, sometimes outspoken, President. Gerwyn Rowlands was for many years a charismatic chairman, his mantle having fallen recently upon John Goss. But since 1948 there has lurked in the background one of Welsh Rugby's great unsung heroes: other long-serving secretaries like Bob Jeremiah of Pontypool, David Price of Swansea, Ken Jones of Llanelli and Allan Benjamin of Neath will not mind my singling out Durbar Lawrie as the most remarkable of their number.

Lawrie took the reins during the difficult years when Bridgend led a nomadic existence in exile from the Brewery Field. After the triumphant return in 1957 he was there to steer the club's revival and steady progress to the front rank. His unsurpassed grasp of administrative detail has ensured crowd control, while an affable personality plus a willingness to take long telephone calls from inquisitive Pressmen makes for excellent public relations. Durbar's weekly 'hymn sheet', full of background facts and statistics, has endeared him to the hacks; but he himself also wields a pen to good effect and has edited two substantial booklets on the life and times of his beloved club. Despite regular rumours of his forthcoming retirement, he is still in office as I write and seems set to remain at the helm into the 'nineties.

Great Days at Brewery Field and Elsewhere

3.5.1975: Bridgend VII 32pts, Cardiff 12pts

In the 'sixties Bridgend took over from Newport as the leading Welsh exponents of the Sevens game. Their approach was coldly efficient, bringing to the mini-game the tactics Cadfan Davies had so successfully imported to the club: being faster around the park, providing intensive support and – above all in Sevens – retaining possession. Ian Lewis, skipper for this their third Snellings victory, was a shrewd thinker who knew when to slow the game down before suddenly thrusting into top gear and allowing wings like diminutive Viv Jenkins and Phil Martell to show their paces.

These two speed-merchants scored four of the winning tries, with Billy Pole and Alan Walters adding two more. Ian Lewis put over four neat conversions.

28.4.1979: Bridgend 18pts, Pontypridd 12pts

Their first appearance in the Schweppes Cup Final could not have provided a better climax to Bridgend's Centenary celebrations. A crowd of 38,000 saw J.P.R. Williams's XV easily contain Pontypridd and run out comfortable winners. This was not a great Final, for Pontypridd by their own confession were a little overawed by the occasion and the strain of playing in front of so big a crowd. The presence of Bridgend's quintet of Internationals ensured that their side suffered no such qualms; but they in turn were enervated by a long and demanding programme of special matches which may have left them somewhat stale.

The game was a personal triumph for centre Steve Fenwick, who raced over for a typical try, converted it, and kicked three penalty goals for a tally of fifteen match-winning points before being forced to the sidelines by a dislocated shoulder. The versatile stand off half Ian Lewis kicked Bridgend's other three points,

Pontypridd replying with a converted try scored by Tom David and a couple of penalties.

26.4.1980: Bridgend 15pts, Swansea 9pts

Bridgend completed a successful defence of the Schweppes Cup in the eightieth minute of an engrossing Final. Swansea dropped their guard for a few fatal seconds, allowing Geoff Davies to snatch a strike against the head. Scrum half Gerald Williams sent Ffrangcon Owen speeding away down the left touchline. The wing dodged a series of tackles, produced a formidable hand-off, and just squeezed in at the corner for a try Steve Fenwick converted with a massive kick. The centre also put over three penalty goals to match those kicked for Swansea by Roger Blyth.

Prop Meredydd James marshalled his pack well and back row forward Gareth Williams was voted man of the match by the Welsh Rugby Writers' Association.

28.10.1981: Bridgend 12pts, Australia 9pts

Most people would rather forget Bridgend's first major fixture against a major overseas touring side. Their eagerly anticipated clash with Graham Mourie's All Blacks was marred by heavy rain and an appalling injury inflicted on J.P.R. Williams by an opposing prop. The result was a 17–6 win for the visitors.

However, their 1981 victory over the Wallabies was a stirring achievement for the mid Glamorgan side. Retirement and defection to the professional game robbed them of two great players in John Williams and Steve Fenwick; but now young Gary Pearce stepped up to give a mature display which nursed his side through against a very determined challenge by the tourists.

John Meadows got the Wallabies' try, Mark Ella converted it and added a penalty late in the game (also missing a relatively straightforward one which could have earned a draw). Meanwhile, however, the twenty-year-old Pearce was on target four times, his final shot from forty-five metres clinching a memorable win.

Heroes of Bridgend

Vivian Jenkins may have represented Oxford University, London Welsh, Kent, the Barbarians, London Counties, Wales and the British Isles, but it was with Bridgend that he got his grounding in club Rugby. This enterprising product of

Llandovery College became the first full back to score a try for Wales when he crossed Ireland's line in 1933 (in his country's 163rd International match). In the course of winning fourteen caps he also ran up thirty-three points for Wales with the boot, and went as vice captain of the 1938 Lions side in South Africa. After retiring he moved into journalism and was the Rugby correspondent of the *Sunday Times*.

A strapping lock during the late 'fifties was **W.R. – 'Roddy' – Evans** who won the first of his thirteen Welsh caps with Cardiff before moving to Bridgend. He toured New Zealand with the Lions, before retiring at the age of twenty-eight to concentrate on a legal career.

Gary Prothero was a specialist blind-side flanker who also made a Lions tour to New Zealand. Beddau-born, he represented Wales eleven times before being forced from the game with a serious eye injury. **Jeff Young** was an able hooker who won twenty-three caps and figured in Wales's Triple Crown and Grand Slam years in 1969 and 1971. Much of his club Rugby was later played with Harrogate, the RAF and London Welsh.

The gifted **John Lloyd** was one of the finest props of his generation, and Bridgend were fortunate to have him as captain during the period when they played some of their best football. A PE teacher trained at the successful Cardiff Training College, he came into the Welsh side at the age of twenty-three and was a fixture at loose head until midway through the 1973 season when back trouble began to interfere with his fitness.

Lloyd, a profound thinker on Rugby techniques and tactics, captained Wales in 1972, a season which could have yielded a Grand Slam had not the match with Ireland been cancelled for political reasons. After retirement he did a stint as coach to the National XV.

Tongwynlais-born **Ian Stephens** was also a technically accomplished prop forward who won respect from all opponents. While on tour with Wales B in 1980, he had the unusual and pleasurable experience of being called to South Africa as a replacement for the injury-hit British Lions.

Between 1975 and 1980, powerfully-built **Steve Fenwick** rose to become Wales's most-capped centre, with thirty appearances. A stocky man, he combined firm defence and penetrative running with a surprising capacity for eeling his way through tight-knit defences for short-range tries. A prodigious place kicker, Fenwick totalled 152 points in appearances for Wales, and was a valuable member of the 1977 Lions in New Zealand.

Near the end of his playing days Fenwick turned professional with the Blue Dragons where he linked up with his business partner, the former Pontypridd skipper Tom David.

CARDIFF RFC

HQ: Cardiff Arms Park
Strip: Cambridge blue and black hoops

In October 1988, Cardiff RFC took the unusual step of calling a Press conference on the morning of their match against Newport. The hacks responded eagerly and partook of generous hospitality from the club chairman, Gary Davies, and senior committee members. Issues touched on included accommodation for journalists,

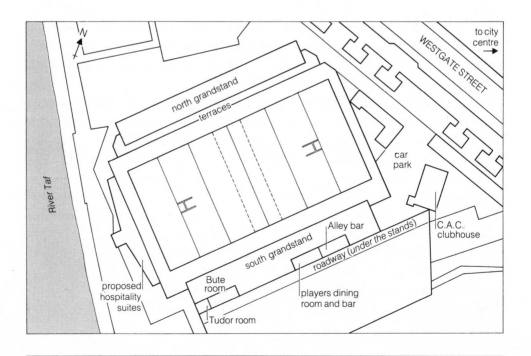

facilities for interviewing players and officials after the final whistle, the media coverage being accorded to the club, and certain current problems such as the difficulty of attracting good new blood.

But underlying the very frank exchanges was an undercurrent of concern, as if Cardiff had become instinctively aware of the need for better public relations in an era when support has to be fought for and Rugby Football, even at the Arms Park, must market itself as never before.

Let it be said straightaway that there are plus points to cheer this great club. Despite the First XV's relatively poor playing record of late, Cardiff continue to be well supported. Their membership is more than satisfactory, and they are fortunate to be the joint owner of the sporting world's most desirable semi-detached properties. However, their claim to be Wales's hotbed of Rugby lore, thought, talent and informed conversation is perhaps less strong than of yore. An older generation of ultra-loyalist, knowledgeable and committed supporters is passing on; bars and clubrooms are not packed to overflowing as once was the case; a question mark hangs over the cherished place in Cardiffians' affection that Cardiff RFC have taken for granted since their foundation in 1876.

Charges of conservatism and an unwillingness to move with the times have been levelled at the committee. There have been major decisions which some thought errors of judgement. Club members and other critics have felt that Cardiff's team selectors have misguidedly kept faith with players who were over the hill rather than pick youngsters with energy and potential for the future.

Such circumstances demand a response, and undoubtedly there will be one. The calling of the Press conference was an example of the club's fresh willingness to ask questions and hear answers. An imaginative scheme has been unfolded for creating a bank of executive boxes at the Taff end of the Cardiff ground which will seek to tap a new market of sponsors looking for venues for entertaining special clients and guests. The scheme, based on that run by big soccer clubs like Manchester United, is calculated to yield a substantial sum from short-term leases and the boxes will be available throughout the year, not just on Cardiff RFC fixture days but also for International occasions on the neighbouring National Ground.

So the giant is stirring – and it can be expected that other imaginative innovations will follow, not all of them perhaps as lucrative as the regular lottery which pulls an annual £60,000 into the Cardiff coffers. The present-day Cardiff committee are aware of the challenge and the measures they will need to take to meet it fully. These, it can confidently be predicted, will be in the best traditions of a club that likes to think of itself as 'the greatest'.

*

Before steam begins to pour from nostrils at Stradey Park, Rodney Parade and other rival establishments, let me quickly add that this accolade is by no means a figment of the late club historian Danny Davies's imagination. The hard-nosed New Zealand critic Terry McLean has written of 'what most of us Down Under consider to be the greatest of all Rugby clubs'. Cardiff, victors over the Springboks in 1907, are the only beaten side to whom South Africa presented a Springbok head (for their valour in defeat in 1951). Des O'Brien testified that 'Cardiff are held in premier esteem in Ireland'. And was it not Carwyn James himself who once admitted, 'when I first came to play for Llanelli we had inherited an inferiority complex as far as Cardiff were concerned'.

What have the Blue and Blacks done to earn such esteem?

They cannot help being the club that represents the capital city of Wales, and that in turn explains why so many outsiders have worn their colours down the years. Early on, immigrants like Frank Hancock and Gwyn Nicholls came in from western England; during the last couple of decades Ken Jones, Gareth Edwards, Barry John, Gareth Davies and Gerald Davies are prime examples of western Welshmen who joined Cardiff and added lustre to the club's achievements – to the general chagrin of the county of Dyfed. Such men, however, have gravitated to Cardiff for career or educational reasons – to brew beer, open laundries, work for finance companies or learn how to teach – so that their moves to the Arms Park have been natural progressions. Such an influx, added to the sturdy products of local District and Youth clubs, has meant that down the years Cardiff have consistently been able to field powerful, attractive teams.

They have the fixtures. Men who want to test their ability at the very highest level know that with Cardiff they can be confident of pitting themselves against Llanelli and Neath, the two most powerful teams in Wales as the 'eighties draw to a close. The great English clubs – Bath, Leicester, Bristol, Harlequins – are all met regularly. Cardiff play the Barbarian tourists in the traditional Easter Saturday festive encounter watched by millions on television. Major touring sides such as the All Blacks and Wallabies invariably come to the Arms Park where a special dispensation allows their matches against Cardiff to take place on the National Ground. And the Blue and Blacks are wanted overseas: South Africa, New Zealand, North America, Zimbabwe and Bangkok have been tour destinations in recent years.

There is, too, an imponderable factor. At Cardiff it is genuinely possible to feel that, important though results may be, it is the game that counts. Cardiff are like any other Rugby club in that they hate losing; but by the time players emerge from the showers any dismay and gloom have evaporated to be replaced by the feeling that, after all, the afternoon's fun in the sun was what really mattered. Hard talking is deferred until Monday night in the interest of hospitality to guests, and controversial refereeing decisions do not become the subject of acrimonious post-match debate.

Not to be overlooked is the Cardiff style. This was delineated in the nineteenth century under the influence of the innovator Frank Hancock, who once threatened to blacklist backs who dropped for goal in preference to running the ball. By and large the Hancock attitude has survived until the present time; Cardiff RFC believe implicitly that Rugby football is a handling game, and even when the immensely powerful Terry Holmes was working the scrummage it could never be alleged that they had resorted to a nine-man game. Thus men who play for Cardiff, and those who watch their teams, can expect the full sense of exhilaration that Rugby at its best offers. Mark Ring, Gerald Cordle and Mike Rayer are current team members who display this Corinthian spirit.

Finally, there is the way that Cardiff look after their players. Almost alone among Welsh clubs the whiff of financial 'incentives' is never to be detected at the Arms Park. Thus the amateur spirit, which despite money-spinning sponsorship, advertising and personal appearances still appeals to the vast majority of Rugby players, goes on flourishing beside the Taff. That is not to say, however, that those representing the club are accorded any but the finest treatment: of his contemporaries Cliff Morgan wrote, '. . .nothing was too good for them. For away fixtures Brice Jenkins made sure that the hotel was first-class and the theatre seats the best in the house. Again, in our two home games each season against age-old rivals Newport we always took the field in brand-new playing-kit and we used new balls. The psychological advantage was amazing!' Such priorities still hold sway in Cardiff RFC and cement commitment and loyalty.

As far as results are concerned, Cardiff have enjoyed four outstanding eras. The twentieth century opened magnificently, with Nicholls, Gabe and Bush combining to clinch victory after colourful victory and a season in 1905–6 which brought just one defeat in thirty-two matches, at the hands of New Zealand. In the late 'thirties Wooller and Cliff Jones were the field marshals, and one can only speculate at the heights the club might have touched had not World War II intervened. But Bleddyn Williams and his contemporaries made up for the lost years with superb Rugby in the late 'forties and early 'fifties: between 1947 and 1958 they won the unofficial Championship six times and were never lower than sixth. These were the years when the old Cardiff Arms Park was often packed to overflowing even for club fixtures, and a game against Newport in 1951 set a world attendance record for a sub-representative match of 48,500 which stood for four decades.

In subsequent years, with Barry John and Gareth Edwards at half back, Cardiff produced brilliant displays without achieving consistency or winning trophies. As the club moved, in 1977, into its second century, people wondered anxiously if there were more great days in store.

With hindsight, it appears to me that the most important single influence on Cardiff at this juncture in their history was the presence of Gerald Davies, who had returned to the city after some years with Cambridge University and London Welsh. A considerable thinker on the game, Davies imported Oxbridge attitudes to Cardiff which reinforced the principles laid down a hundred years before by Frank Hancock. After the retirement of Edwards and John – match-winners in themselves – there gradually came a return to fifteen-man Rugby in which all players were expected to become involved and to contribute. The Schweppes Cup eluded the teams Davies led; but he had laid foundations.

Again the club enjoyed good fortune. The burly, skilful John Scott, a Devonian, transferred to Cardiff from Rosslyn Park and took over where Gerald Davies had left off. His contribution was to bring power and discipline to the club's forward play, so that the new generation of gifted backs like Holmes and Gareth Davies got time and space in which to run and pass. Scott, a man who did not suffer fools gladly on committee or in the media, was a captain for whom his players' interests came first, and under him morale was high. His successor Alan Phillips was cast in a similar mould; Roger Beard was a taciturn but able coach; selection and player management became the responsibility of the urbane and approachable C.D. Williams.

Thus a fourth grand era ensued. After failing to win the Schweppes Cup in nine campaigns (and experiencing humiliation at Llanelli's hands in the 1973 Final) Cardiff triumphed five times in the 1980s and won the Championship in 1982. In between-times the club's Sevens sides took the Snelling trophy on three occasions. There was heavy scoring, unsurpassed entertainment – and a great sense of pride in achievement.

But, lest they forget: the late Danny Davies warned in his *History* published in 1976, 'A club is not "great" merely because of its age or periods of brilliance. It must have a traditional standard of Rugby in the spirit of the game, pleasing to both its players and public. It must retain the admiration of its adversaries for its standard of sportsmanship whilst at the same time retaining its hospitable and administrative reputation in the Rugby world.'

Gary Davies, secretary Alun Priday, Colin Howe, C.D. Williams, Tony Williams and the rest of the committee are aware of that reputation. It is something they will guard jealously.

Great Club Days at Cardiff Arms Park

1.1.1907: Cardiff 17pts, South Africa 0pts

Cardiff made up for the single lapse of concentration which had cost them a victory against New Zealand in 1905 by overwhelming Paul Roos's Springboks. On a mud-bound pitch with a south-westerly blasting in from over the Taff they ran in four breathtaking tries without reply, Bert Winfield rubbing in their superiority with a conversion and penalty goal.

Though he was by now a veteran, and had rather reluctantly emerged from retirement at the request of the Wales and Cardiff selectors, this was Gwyn Nicholls's match. Soon after the kick off a long throw reached him some thirty-five yards from the tourists' line. Accelerating through the midfield defence with a swing of the hips he left the cover for dead and crossed wide out without a hand being put on him. Reggie Gibbs, John Williams and Rhys Gabe were also try scorers as the South Africans went down to only their second defeat on British soil.

27.9.1947: Cardiff 11pts, Australia 3pts

A 40,000 crowd came to the Arms Park to see the glittering Cardiff side of the day take on Bill McLean's Wallabies, who had acquired a reputation for an over-physical approach. The club's mastery on the day began in the front row, where the 'miners' union' – Maldwyn James, Cliff Davies and W.G. Jones – were too good for their opposite numbers Nick Shehadie, Walter Dawson and Bob McMaster. Ably supported by Roy Roberts, Les Manfield and Bill Tamplin they gave Tanner and the backs enough possession to make sure of victory.

20.10.1951: Cardiff 9pts, South Africa 11pts

The Fourth Springboks are remembered by many as the most gifted and capable touring side to have visited the British Isles. After an early injury to skipper Basil Kenyon they were led by the outstanding number eight forward Hennie Muller, who inspired his men to a quintet of Test victories against the Home Countries and

France on a tour which contained only one defeat, by London Counties. That apart, their hardest game outside the Tests was at Cardiff where Jack Matthews's side lost by just two points. This was the occasion when the visitors handed over a Springbok head, normally reserved for teams which beat them, in recognition of the Welshmen's great struggle.

Minutes before time Cardiff were in the lead 9–8. Though South Africa had scored two tries, one of them converted, grafting by the home pack allied to tremendous tackling in the midfield had checked their momentum – and created chances for Bill Tamplin to kick two penalty goals and Bleddyn Williams to grab a try. As time ran out, the 53,000-strong crowd thought the South Africans, pinned uncomfortably in their own 25, must be doomed to defeat in this fourth match of their tour.

Then it was that the astute stand off half Hannes Brewis put in the most crucial tactical kick of his career, floating a long ball on the wind towards the opposite corner flag. Left wing 'Chum' Ochse set off in pursuit as the defence turned desperately towards the danger zone. His twinkling feet outstripped everyone, including Cardiff full back Frank Trott, to get a match-winning touch-down inches in from touch. The conversion failed, but this was a marvellous climax to an enthralling game of Rugby football.

21.11.1953: Cardiff 8pts, New Zealand 3pts

Cardiff made up for their narrow defeat by South Africa with a win which completed a hat trick against touring sides from the Dominions. It was a great performance; people were to say later that Bob Stuart's team was the weakest All Black ensemble to visit Britain, but though New Zealand sides are sometimes limited, they are never weak – and this one contained the biggest pack of forwards that had ever represented them on tour.

Bleddyn Williams was his team's inspiration, but the man of the match was Sid Judd, soon to die tragically of a blood disease. Not only did he bring the best out of his smaller eight, he also got the vital first score, chasing Gwyn Rowlands' cross kick and crashing in close to the posts for a converted try.

After a Ron Jarden penalty for New Zealand, Cardiff edged further ahead. This time brilliant interplay between Cliff Morgan, Bleddyn Williams and Alun Thomas outmanoeuvred the midfield defence, and even the great full back Bob Scott could not lay a hand on scorer Gwyn Rowlands.

The remaining fifty-five minutes were a memorable stalemate as the forwards grimly slogged it out. New Zealand increased their forward effort and Judd's pack were never again able to give their brilliant backs a clear run – though hooker Geoff Beckingham stole two tight heads late in the game which robbed the tourists of good chances to level accounts.

21.1.1978: Pontypool 11pts, Cardiff 16pts

With four Lions in their pack, Pontypool were favourites to win this Schweppes Cup tie and swiftly went ahead 7–0. This was when Gerald Davies produced one of the finest individual displays ever from a Cardiff captain in a club match and led his side to a win that was in the end comfortable.

The statisticians say that the visitors secured good ball on only five occasions. Such was the form of their back division, however, that four tries resulted from these crumbs of possession, Davies being the scorer each time. The most memorable was a 50-metre sprint down the touchline, fending off the buffetings of the Pontypool cover and finally darting beyond the full back's reach. Though Cardiff were eliminated from the competition at the semi final stage, their away victory on this day remains one of the greatest performances in Schweppes Cup history.

11.4.1981: Cardiff 14pts, Bridgend 6pts
28.4.1984: Cardiff 24pts, Neath 19pts
26.4.1986: Cardiff 28pts, Newport 21pts

At last, in the 'eighties, Cardiff emerged as a force in the Schweppes Cup competition. Their first victims were Bridgend, who arrived at the Arms Park in 1981 as favourites. Bridgend, soon to clinch the Championship, were the holders and had arrived at the Final without having a try scored against them. But in the war of attrition which ensued they were outgunned by a Cardiff pack inspired by John Scott and nursed forward by Terry Holmes.

Bob Lakin scored first after Bridgend had failed to hold their own line out ball, pouncing for a try which helped him to win the man of the match award. In the second half a brilliant loop move by Gareth Davies, who also put over important place kicks, was carried on by full back Glyn Davies and try scorer Neil Hutchings.

Cardiff were to defend the trophy successfully in an unsatisfactory repeat against Bridgend decided by a single try, but two years later a tremendous challenge by Neath brought the very best out of them in what was considered to be the best Final since 1972 and the start of the competition. Neath played carefree attacking Rugby against a side which looked somewhat stale and wore the mantle of favourites uneasily.

Owen Golding and Gerald Cordle were Cardiff's try scorers, but the man of the match was the All Blacks' scrum half Gareth Jones. Unimpressed by the nearby presence of Terry Holmes, he first electrified the crowd with an 80-metre touchline sprint which was just halted on the flag by Cardiff's cover. Not to be thwarted, however, Jones darted away from the set scrum that followed and nipped over for a classic try. David Jacob scored twice, but four penalty goals by Gareth Davies put his side just out of reach.

Cardiff's 1986 meeting with their old rivals Newport was over as a contest early in the second half when they extended their lead to 22–6. As the throttle was eased back, their opponents got face-saving scores, but the final try count was four-three in Cardiff's favour including a first ever hat-trick in a Final, scored by Adrian Hadley.

In his last appearance for his club in a major fixture Gareth Davies kicked three conversions and two penalty goals. But with his departure, and the defection to Rugby League of Terry Holmes, it seemed that the club's fourth 'golden era' was drawing to a close. Perhaps Cardiff's 16–15 victory over Swansea in the 1987 final was the drawing-down of the curtain.

Heroes of Cardiff Arms Park

Choosing heroes from Cardiff's roll of honour is like picking out individual stars from a galaxy. However, there can be little disagreement about the club's first great man. **Frank Hancock**, one of four footballing brothers from Wiveliscombe in Somerset, came to Cardiff to join the family brewery. In 1884 he involuntarily inaugurated the four three quarter system: pulled in as replacement centre for a match at Cheltenham, he played so well that Cardiff wished to retain him the following week – which they did at the expense of one of the pack, fielding eight forwards and seven backs as opposed to nine and six.

A brilliant 'corkscrew runner' with good skills, and an advocate of open Rugby, Hancock was one of Cardiff's most successful captains. He led them through the outstanding campaign of 1885–86 which brought only one reverse, in the final game against Moseley. At a time when national qualifications were blurred he won four caps for Wales.

Percy Bush was an early Rhondda Valley export to Cardiff RFC, joining the club in 1899 and reaching his peak as captain in 1905. Besides dazzling footwork and speed off the mark, he is remembered for his cheek and confidence on the field amounting almost to arrogance. The latter trait may have let him down when he led Cardiff against the 1905 All Blacks: casualness in dealing with a loose ball over the line allowed the New Zealanders to steal a try which gave them a 10–8 win.

Rhys Gabe won his place in the catalogue of Welsh Rugby 'greats' for the tackle on Bob Deans which prevented New Zealand getting a draw against Wales in 1905 and plunged them to their sole defeat. But he can also claim to be the only player to have received possession from David Lloyd George. The then President of the Board of Trade kicked off in a match against Blackheath straight into the hands of Gabe, who claimed a mark!

In the 'twenties a number of Cardiff schools turned from soccer to Rugby, thus revitalising the inflow of local talent to the Arms Park. **Harry Bowcott** was the outstanding product of this new trend, joining the club in 1926 and winning the first of his eight caps in 1929. He also toured New Zealand with the 1930 British Lions as a stand off half, where his polish and composure won many plaudits. In later life Bowcott emerged as an outstanding selector whose excellent identification of potential in players underwrote many well-chosen Welsh XVs.

After the Second World War, Cardiff's back divisions caught the eye with incisive, free-flowing handling that produced both high success and matchless entertainment. But the backs' brilliance was under-written by power forward play in which the immense **Ewart Tamplin** stood out. A fine line out forward and mauler, he was also a goal kicker who could thump the old, heavy leather balls great distances. An able and well-loved contemporary was the prop **Cliff Davies** who could sing like an angel – the 'bard of Kenfig' they called him – prop like a stoker and run like the wind: the outstanding moment in a sixteen-cap International career was his Twickenham try of 1950 which helped set Wales on a Grand Slam trail.

Billy Cleaver was the tactician who nursed these forwards upfield and kept Cardiff – and Wales – going forward. An early master of the screw kick, he won fourteen caps between 1947 and 1950 when he retired, some thought prematurely. Outside him **Dr Jack Matthews** was the 'hit-man' of his day, a sprint champion whose crash-tackling was every bit as spectacular as his scything breaks. These two, plus Cliff Davies, Bleddyn Williams and **Rex Willis** were Cardiff's representatives on the 1950 Lions tour of Australia and New Zealand.

Willis is remembered as the 'minder' of Cliff Morgan. But he was much more: a tough, brave player who never gave his stand off half bad ball and was always prepared to stoop before the flying boots of opposing forwards on the rampage. Another Rhondda Valley product, he won twenty-one caps and was on fifteen winning sides. Willis acted successfully as a Barbarian committee-man in Wales during the 'seventies and 'eighties.

One of Cardiff's brightest stars from the west was **D.K. Jones**, known as 'Ken bach' to distinguish him from the Newport wing. A short, stocky figure, he was strongly built and could generate tremendous pace in midfield. His 1962 try for the Lions against South Africa was one of the great individual Test scores of all time, beating the Springbok cover defence for pace and stepping deftly inside the full back to cross the line. **Keith Rowlands** was a fine club captain who toured with the Lions and won four caps; but it is as an administrator that he has made a mark latterly as the International Board's first full-time secretary.

The grinning face of **Maurice Richards** graced the front cover of the new *Welsh Brewers' Rugby Annual for Wales* in 1969–70 to salute his record-equalling four tries against England during that Triple Crown season. This boosted his try-scoring ratio to seven in nine International appearances and made him a ready target for the professional game which duly snapped him up in 1969. Like his successor from the Rhondda, **John Bevan**, Richards was one of the most powerful wings ever to represent Wales; but whereas the latter, a British Lion in 1971, relied on speed and physical confrontation Richards was equipped with a truly fantastic body-swerve and change of direction to baffle opponents. These two were unerring finishers for Cardiff in the era when Edwards and John carved out the openings.

Gareth Davies was one of the most balanced and elegant stand off halves ever to represent Cardiff and Wales. His problem was that onlookers assumed that he could automatically step into the boots of Barry John and Phil Bennett – conveniently forgetting that his predecessors were surrounded by men of outstanding ability who could take the pressure off a stand off half. Thus memories of Davies at play are most treasured in the Cardiff club, whereas his International career was studded with disappointment and setbacks, and he was always vulnerable to challenge from less gifted men than himself. His line-kicking, however, was supreme, and he often dropped match-winning goals.

The affection in which **Terry Holmes** is held at Cardiff is attested by the action portrait of him which commands an honoured place on the clubhouse wall despite his defection to Rugby League in 1985. He won twenty-five caps for Wales and made 195 appearances for Cardiff, with a phenomenal strike-rate of 123 tries.

A quietly-spoken, gentle man off the field, Holmes was a tiger on it, always eager to duel with big back row forwards. Collisions with such men led to a series of injuries in his later years which eventually brought his career to a spluttering conclusion. But no try-line was safe when Holmes was five yards distant from it.

At seventeen, Devonian **John Scott** became the youngest Englishman to play in an International trial, winning a first cap against France in 1978. It was Cardiff's good fortune that he quickly moved from Rosslyn Park to sharpen his game in the hurly-burly of the big Welsh circuit.

In the 'eighties, when he captained the club for a record four seasons, Scott was a dominant figure at number eight and occasionally lock forward. Allied to a considerable bulk were ball skills of a high order plus tactical awareness and leadership qualities which made him a great all-round clubman. Despite being on the periphery as far as England's selectors were concerned, he made thirty-four appearances for his country and is their most capped number eight forward. A stalwart lieutenant of Scott, who took over the captaincy successfully from the Englishman was **Alan Phillips**. This high-scoring hooker certainly deserved more than the eighteen caps he won between 1979 and 1987. **Robert Norster** was a third fine forward of this vintage and probably the world's outstanding line out jumper of the mid 'eighties.

Adrian Hadley undoubtedly belongs in the long list of the greatest Cardiff players. He was the most unassuming of men, on and off the field – except when he became involved in the action. Then he could produce every trick in the wing's book including a baffling pace-change and a big swerve. Excellent hands made Hadley a fine finisher as was underlined by his try against Australia in 1987 and the pair he scored at Twickenham in 1989 shortly before turning professional.

Finally, there is the multi-talented **Mark Ring** who gravitated to senior Rugby early in the 'eighties after outstanding seasons with the club's youth XV. A back in the great Welsh mould, he has nevertheless suffered injury and career setbacks. His second severe accident to a knee in the autumn of 1988 not only sidelined him at a time when he might have been expected to reach full flower as a player; it also robbed the struggling Welsh XV of a centre with genuine penetrative powers and originality – a man for whom the national coach John Ryan 'had great plans'.

Ring's great expectation was to succeed Gareth Davies and serve Cardiff as a stand off half. The club's curious reluctance to persevere with him in his favourite position undoubtedly disappointed him considerably, prompting his brilliant year in Gwent with Pontypool and some discreet enquiries about his worth to Rugby League. His return to the Arms Park fold in 1989 was generally welcomed, and it seems likely that after recovering from his latest operation he has several more years of good Rugby Football left in him.

LLANELLI RFC

HQ: Stradey Park
Strip: Scarlet

The affection in which I hold Stradey Park is considerable – even though I nearly met my death on its terrace steps. Several media colleagues also count themselves lucky to have escaped with their lives after the terrifying occurrence of December 12, 1970.

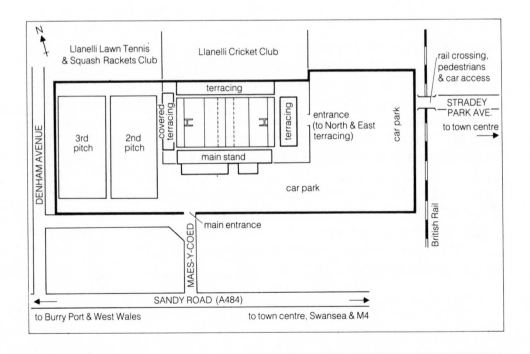

At the time I was in my first season as a match commentator on televised Rugby for BBC Wales. Llanelli Rugby Football Club were in the van of progress, as usual, and had commendably agreed to the suspension from the grandstand roof of a deck for TV crews and equipment (previously coverage had been effected from the popular bank, giving unsatisfactory pictures shot into the sun). This rather makeshift structure hung some thirty feet above the enclosure, directly opposite the half way line. The position afforded, and still affords, the best viewpoint in Britain and possibly the world for coverage of Rugby football.

That day Stradey Park was staging the Welsh Rugby Union's first International Trial. The wooden TV deck, held in place by scaffolding, supported two cameras and an assortment of personnel who included two cameramen, the recently retired Wales skipper Brian Price who was the 'second voice' providing expert comment (and must have wished later that he had stayed in the game!), floor managers, sound engineers, riggers and myself. All of us were there legitimately and the safety regulations were scrupulously observed.

Some minutes before kick-off there was a creak from the structure, loud enough to prompt spectators in the enclosure to look up nervously and seek alternative viewpoints. Checks were set in motion while the TV team completed its important pre-match preparations. I carried out my own final scrutiny of the names and records of the players who were down to take part in the match.

Just as the Reds and Whites trotted onto Stradey's turf one end of our deck of planks slid from the grip of the scaffold screws, tipping us helplessly downwards. I was pitched forward and in a trice found myself tumbling head first towards the concrete steps below.

It is not true that your whole life whizzes before your mind's eye at such moments. I had just time to reflect gloomily, 'What a futile way to die,' when I bumped against the shoulder of a solitary spectator who had not heard the creak minutes earlier and doubtless couldn't believe his luck at having found such a fine viewpoint just before the kick off. I often wonder who this person was, for his presence checked my fall and certainly saved my life. Friendly hands helped me from the turmoil of shattered equipment and groaning colleagues, and after a short rest I watched the Trial from a safe seat in the grandstand along with those who had come to earth more or less in one piece. A senior cameraman, Tom Blake, was not so lucky and underwent operations for severe head injuries at Morriston Hospital in the ensuing days. My chief discomfiture was stiffness and bruising that kept me confined to bed for a fortnight.

That same weekend the deaths from trampling and suffocation of many spectators on an exit staircase at Ibrox Park in Glasgow monopolised the headlines, so that the Llanelli incident did not receive quite the public going-over it certainly merited. As a result, however, television organisations tightened their surveillance of gantries and decks erected for crews and cameras. The nuts and bolts of existing ones were examined for rust and corrosion, while new installations were subjected to rigorously up-graded safety regulations. At Stradey Park a permanent structure, bolted and welded to the grandstand, now accommodates media folk in complete safety.

The ladder leading to that gantry is steep; climbing it often put me in mind of a crack which former referee 'Larry' Lamb has used in after-dinner speeches to Rugby audiences: the higher you climb in life the more your shortcomings are exposed.

Certainly visiting commentators on their way aloft are exceedingly vulnerable to the acid tongues of regulars in the enclosure. As I puffed and hauled my way upwards my ears were frequently assailed by shouts of 'bluddy Blue and Black' (Cardiff) or 'Poola' (Pontypool), implying that my impartiality was not what it ought to have been. From that position it was difficult to swivel round and explain to the crowd below that bias is in the minds of the listeners. They would only have laughed anyway.

Such good-natured heckling stems from a passion for the game in Scarlet supporters which is surpassed only by their loyalty to Llanelli RFC. They are genially aware of their single-mindedness exemplified in the title of Stradey's fan club, 'Cyclops'. In their time they have thrown mud at referees, assaulted policemen, and been asked by the club committee to cut out bad language on the terraces. Their allegiance can reach heights of perversity, as in 1980 when club secretary Ken Jones said that the playing record was the worst for twenty years – only for the treasurer to report a record income of £103,000.

There are good reasons for such unswerving devotion. Firstly, although a doughty soccer team plays at Stebonheath Park, Llanelli is one of the few towns of its size in Britain without a team competing in the Football League. Thus Stradey Park, visited by Britain's top Rugby teams and all important touring sides, stands alone as a major venue for spectator sport.

The club is also a focal point for the enthusiasm of the whole of west Wales. It draws players both from an inner ring of satellites such as Felinfoel, Bynea, Tumble and Hendy, and from further afield in the sizeable county of Dyfed. Roy Bergiers from Carmarthen, Bancyfelin-born Delme Thomas and Peter Morgan of Haverfordwest are examples of men from the rural west who have served Llanelli with distinction in recent years. And when such players pull on the Scarlet jersey, supporters journey far for the special thrill of seeing local heroes perform at Stradey.

Perhaps the most important factor in the business of winning and retaining support is the style of play Llanelli embrace. They are not invincible. Occasionally they appear indifferent to their fate. They can be careless and slipshod. But they are never, never dull to watch. They accept that often a forward slog has to be won before they can give rein to their attacking instincts, but running and handling remain the ideals which are handed on and grasped eagerly as generation succeeds generation. And thanks to the vision of their elders, coaches – like Gareth Jenkins, currently in charge – are granted freedom to approach match play the Scarlet way.

Stradey Park, first used for Rugby in 1879, lies a mile to the west of Llanelli's town centre. New roads are easing the traffic strain, but nevertheless on big match days the buses and cars can but crawl along from Hendy and Gorseinon in the east, Tumble to the north and Burry Port in the west. Drivers are canny enough to start early; but they have no fears about being able to park once they reach the stadium: many years ago the Rugby club acquired the surrounding acres of land, so that vehicles by the hundred can lie patiently parked while the great athletic dramas take place inside the ground.

Between the cars spectators weave their way, a steady stream that starts two hours before kick-off and flows ceaselessly onto the north terrace overlooking the cricket field and the banking at Stradey's eastern, or town, end. This is where the small boys congregate, encroaching onto the turf as play progresses in the hope of being able to seize the ball and toss it back to the players after a conversion or penalty kick at goal. The terrace at the Pwll end, covered in 1955 for £400, fills up with visitors from Trimsaran, Pontyates, Pontyberem and points west.

For those eager to spot celebrities, collect autographs from famous players or simply enjoy a gossip with pals, the area behind the grandstand is the place to be. Coaches pull up here with visiting teams and supporters, while the Llanelli fifteen for the match park their cars and slip unobtrusively through the players' entrance. Here knots of friends and enthusiasts congregate, often receiving a welcome from club officials like Peter Rees, Elvet Jones, Marlston Morgan and long-serving secretary Ken Jones. Tickets change hands – legitimately; this is not tout country.

Match-day tension mounts slowly but perceptibly in premises that are little short of palatial. The public bars are spacious and comfortable. Members and season ticket holders can choose from a number of ample rooms where conversation bubbles buoyantly on draughts of Buckleys and Felinfoel, the local brews. VIPs may attend the Carwyn James Room which can be reserved for the dispensing of private hospitality. Nearby is a warren of smaller dens where other guests can be entertained.

Another reception suite which these days proves highly attractive to sponsors is the trophy room, its walls and glass cases flush with the archives of this extraordinary club. Here are the records and relics of the renowned, their portraits on canvas, their great moments captured by the camera. Here, on permanent display, is the back page from the *Western Mail* of 1 November 1972 celebrating the Scarlets' victory over New Zealand. Here, too is a handsome tinted photograph of HRH the Prince of Wales seated in the grandstand when he came to see his Royal Regiment of Wales play Llanelli. Outside, the history of Stradey Park is all about confrontation and conflict; but the trophy room is a peaceful inner sanctum.

The players' changing rooms are insulated from these spectator areas by glass doors. When they swing open to allow access to match officials, the rhythmic stamping of studs on tiling can be heard as the teams go through their warm-up routines. These quarters, too, are bright and modern, with showerbaths and a massage table. The visitors' room is at the far end of the corridor, so that the rival camps are spared the embarrassment of having their pre-match pep-talks overheard. Close by are private rooms where the teams can unwind with a cup of tea or something stronger after the final whistle and exchange compliments with their opponents. These fine premises, along with the upstairs dining hall, date back to 1965. The £21,000 bill, a fortune in those days, is an example of the priority the Llanelli club has always given to the welfare and comfort of the protagonists – the men who provide the afternoon's sport and spectacle.

Surmounting all these nooks and crannies is the grandstand, extended in 1970 to seat 2650 people – ample accommodation, though Pressmen tend to feel that provision for them is somewhat cramped. Patrons look out on a fine stretch of turf which falls ever so slightly from east to west, the direction in which the Scarlets prefer to play in the second half. The popular terrace opposite is a colourful sight when full, and towering above the pitch's four corners are the magnificent floodlights, installed in 1977 and still probably the best at any Rugby Union club ground. Uncertainty seems to surround the official crowd capacity of Stradey Park and even what is the best attendance ever recorded; but there may have been 25,000 crammed in to see the defeat of the 1972 All Blacks.

Wherever you stand or sit, you are assured of a good view of the contest. And young fans steal a march on the grown-ups, for Llanelli is one of the very few venues (offhand I can think of no other) where small boys are allowed to race across the pitch at half time to beg autographs from the players. Mostly they are ignored, but their enthusiasm never evaporates. And the Scarlets' administrators are shrewd; they know in whose hands the fortunes of the club will one day lie.

There is a final point to be made about the Scarlets, and that concerns their resilience under volleys of economic slings and arrows. Even late in the last century, the smoke-stack industries' heyday, whole work forces could be thrown onto the dole as factories fell victim to tariff adjustments made in far-off markets like the United States. Back in the 'twenties and 'thirties scarcely a season went by without the departure of leading players who, as victims of successive slumps, were only too glad to accept lucrative offers to turn professional and go north. Just over a decade ago there were more bad experiences, from which few were immune – even the great Phil Bennett found himself jobless when Duport shut down. Recently the town has reeled before the loss of eight hundred jobs through the demise of a car plant.

Located on the perimeter of British industrial activity, Llanelli's economy is certainly a vulnerable one. For young men with families, recessions mean long periods of anxiety and even desperation.

Discernibly, there are days when such knife-edge fears are reflected in the feverish brilliance of the Scarlets' play: the response of bold men to troubled times.

Llanelli's Greatest Days

20.1.1970: Llanelli 9pts, South Africa 10pts

Many Springboks of different generations agree that the try by Alan Richards in this game can claim to be the finest scored against one of their tour sides in this country – and 20,000 Welsh spectators would not disagree.

It came fifteen minutes into the second half with Llanelli trailing 6–3 and playing towards the town end. Dimunitive centre John Thomas began it by charging down a tactical kick near his team's 25-yard line. Here is the roll of honour commemorating the Scarlets who, with characteristic exuberance, developed a superb counter-attack: Clive John, Gwyn Ashby, Roy Mathias, Selwyn Williams (replacement), Brian Butler, Ashby again, Stuart Gallacher, Alan John, Clive John again, Selwyn Williams again, Roy Mathias again.

Mathias's touchline sprint was ably supported by Selwyn Williams, John Thomas, Arwyn Reynolds and Alan John. The latter's was the overhead scoring pass to wing Alan Richards.

Phew!

A second unconverted try and a penalty by the Scarlets were, alas, insufficient to yield a coveted first victory over South Africa, for whom raider Jan Ellis grabbed two converted tries.

31.10.1972: Llanelli 9pts, New Zealand 3pts

This was 'the day the pubs ran dry,' to quote Max Boyce.

The Scarlets had met New Zealand four times since 1924, failing narrowly on each occasion. After Ian Kirkpatrick's All Blacks opened their 1972–73 tour with a 39–12 victory at Gloucester it seemed that the second challengers, Llanelli, would be ruthlessly brushed aside as the visitors cranked up their game.

Nonetheless, on a calm, overcast autumn afternoon, Stradey Park was still bursting at the seams. Could the impossible dream become reality and light up the Scarlets' Centenary season?

In skipper Delme Thomas and flank forward Derek Quinnell the home team had Lions who had tasted victory over the All Blacks in New Zealand the previous year; not to mention the coach to that famous side, Carwyn James. After the latter had delivered a pre-match pep-talk in his own quiet, under-stated style, Thomas took over to stoke the fire in the team's belly and declare that he would exchange all the honours Rugby football had given him for victory in this match. His words brought tears to the eyes of his more emotional listeners.

There is no doubt that Llanelli's supercharged opening caught the tourists off balance and the decisive score came before ten minutes had gone by. A curving penalty attempt by Phil Bennett bounced down off a post to New Zealand scrum half Lyn Colling. He delayed his clearance a fatal tenth of a second for Roy Bergiers to charge it down and pounce for a sensational try which Bennett converted. The All Blacks looked shaken and disconcerted as Llanelli pressed home their advantage, actively seeking confrontation with their burly opponents, tackling and falling on the ball like men possessed. The visitors' full back Joe Karam put one penalty over after 25 minutes but missed another, so that his side still trailed 6–3 at the break.

The second half was tremendously hard fought, with New Zealand throwing everything in to avoid defeat and the big crowd perpetually on tenterhooks. Even when Andy Hill put over a giant goal from the half way line there were still ten minutes left in which New Zealand might have snatched victory or at least a draw; and in this torrid period Llanelli were magnificently served by the defensive kicking of Phil Bennett. Finally the tourists had no ideas left, and their stomach for the fight was gone. Referee Mike Titcomb blew for time – and the celebrations began. Supporters flooded onto the pitch to chair off Delme Thomas, Ray Gravell, Chico Hopkins and the rest. Vast red dragon banners were waved triumphantly over the half way line. Impromptu choirs sang, 'Who beat the All Blacks – Good old Sospan Fach!' In defeat New Zealand manager Ernie Todd was gracious and spoke of Llanelli's 'fantastic team performance'.

Though he had set a club record of 362 points the previous year which was to survive until 1986, this was certainly Andy Hill's finest hour. A wing who could carve out his own chances as well as rounding off moves dependably, he played 454 games for Llanelli before retiring in 1979 with a career points record of 2577. Had his defence measured up to his outstanding qualities in attack he must surely have been capped by Wales.

28.4.1973: Llanelli 30pts, Cardiff 7pts
27.4.1974: Llanelli 12pts, Aberavon 10pts
26.4.1975: Llanelli 15pts, Aberavon 6pts
24.4.1976: Llanelli 16pts, Swansea 4pts

After a surprise 1972 reverse at the hands of Neath in the first Final of modern times, Llanelli proceeded to win the Welsh Rugby Union Challenge Cup, latterly known as the Schweppes Cup, for the next four seasons on the trot. They thereby set a record which it is impossible to envisage being equalled, let alone broken.

The first of the wins was the most flamboyant. A mediocre Cardiff side felt the backlash of the Scarlets' defeat twelve months earlier and went down by what is still the biggest losing margin in a Final, 23 points. Good goal-kicking by Phil Bennett edged his side ahead by half time, after which Llanelli cut loose with three fine tries by Ray Gravell, John Williams and Hefin Jenkins.

Their 1974 triumph was the most unexpected. An agonising decision had to be taken by four of the Scarlets' stars, Phil Bennett, Roy Bergiers, J.J. Williams and Tom David: should they play and risk an injury which would keep them out of the forthcoming Lions tour of South Africa? Or should they withdraw from the Final, leaving their side short of experience and flair?

Helped, no doubt, by a wink and a nod from their magnanimous club committee, the four opted out. And when Aberavon's John Bevan engineered a try for Steve Roper after seven minutes, people in the crowd smiled knowingly to each other –

not even Llanelli could overcome so great a handicap. Now the Scarlets showed their great character and paraded their strength in depth. Youthful deputy Bernard Thomas did Bennett's number ten jersey proud at stand off half, nursing his pack magnificently, while schoolboys David Nicholas and John Walters were brave in the face of Aberavon's rampant attacks. Allan Martin kept the Wizards in contention to the end with two penalty goals, but four by Andy Hill ensured that the Cup stayed at Stradey Park. If not a victory in the flamboyant Llanelli tradition, 1974 at least showed that the club's success was not merely a matter of star quality.

The following year Llanelli again saw off Aberavon, this time by a nine-point margin, and returned to the National Ground in 1976 to complete their run of four Cup Final triumphs in a row by defeating Swansea 16–4. Phil Bennett, Ray Gravell and John Williams had played in the Welsh Grand Slam side, and their winners' tankards were the icing on a splendid cake of a season.

The Scarlets' 26-match run of Cup wins was ended in 1977 by Cardiff, who beat them 25–15 in the third round.

27.4.1985: Llanelli 15pts, Cardiff 14pts

After that tremendous run of success in the 'seventies, who could have imagined that Llanelli would wait nine long years for their next Schweppes Cup triumph. When it came it was doubly sweet.

This was a classic confrontation: West versus East; Llanelli's fifteen-man potential versus opponents who would seek control through a strong pack and halves Terry Holmes and Gareth Davies. And as the end of proper time arrived it seemed that the percentage approach had paid off, with Cardiff ahead at 14–12. But Phil May's side had hung on in there, and in the forty-first minute won a desperately contested scrum on the Blue and Blacks' line. Gary Pearce's drop kick headed wide of the far post before drifting in inches over the bar to give his team an unexpected but heroically deserved win.

5.11.1985: Llanelli 31pts, Fiji 28pts

Long ago, Stradey Park staged a number of International matches. That of 1893 between Wales and Ireland had spectators scratching their heads: in a 3–0 victory which brought them the first Triple Crown in their history, the home team fielded four three quarters against Ireland's three. The experiment became permanent and was soon adopted by other nations.

Since those early days the Rugby football served up for enthusiasts in the west has seldom lacked innovation and inventiveness. There have been great games, tremendous results, incredible feats by individuals. But eclipsing the rest with its sheer improbability was the score-line of Tuesday, 5 November 1985.

The Fijian tourists that autumn were the usual blend of flair and fallibility, but had strung together three impressive wins in a row before their fixture at Stradey. They took this buoyancy into a dynamic first-half display, including four tries in a twelve-minute burst, and built what looked like an unassailable lead of 28–4. Two of the scores came from interceptions on their own line and thrilling sprints by Jimi Damu and Peli Tuvula.

Skipper Phil May decided that enough was enough and perceptibly tightened the Scarlets' tactics. Even when he and Anthony Buchanan drove in for tries after forward surges, few thought that the huge deficit would be wiped out, but the sturdy little stand off half Gary Pearce had other ideas. His precise tactical kicking confined the tourists to their own half where, when their resistance wavered, he put over a series of penalties, conversions and a dropped goal totalling fifteen vital points. Thus with only minutes left Llanelli were a mere three points adrift: the unbelievable was within reach. The Fijians could do nothing to reverse the tide and conceded a last-second try by Alun Hopkins that clinched an astonishing result.

Hero Gary Pearce, who won three caps without quite fulfilling his early promise, set a new club scoring record of 420 points that season. He signed for Hull RL club in autumn 1986.

7.5.1988: Llanelli 29pts, Neath 9pts

Again Llanelli's opponents were slight favourites – but this time the Scarlets, for whom Jonathan Davies was now the master-tactician at stand off half, cut Neath to shreds and sewed up a record sixth Cup triumph with tries by Ieuan Evans, Laurance Delaney and Gary Jones.

The 56,000 attendance broke the record for a club game which had stood since 1951 when 48,500 watched a Cardiff-Newport match.

Stradey's Heroes

Albert Jenkins gained fourteen caps as a centre in the 'twenties. A dockworker who regularly did a Saturday morning shift at the quayside before reporting to Stradey Park, he nevertheless resisted a series of enormous cash baits dangled in front of him by Rugby League clubs – maybe because of the attacks of homesickness from which he was said to suffer.

Crowds loved his forceful running and devastating hand-off. A buzz of expectation rose, too, when he dropped for goal, sometimes from the half way line.

R.H. (Rhys) Williams was one of the finest lock forwards to represent Wales or any other country. A tendency to stoop disguised his full height of six feet four inches and a breadth of frame that was power-packed. He matured young, and at twenty-one was tangling with the mighty Fourth Springboks in Llanelli's gallant but unrewarded struggle of 1951.

'R.H.' was a key lock on the exciting 1955 tour of South Africa in which he gained four Test caps for the Lions. He subsequently travelled with the less successful side of 1959 in New Zealand, before announcing his retirement. He played twenty-three times for Wales.

Of late he has been a selector in a volatile and unpredictable period of the game in Wales.

Terry Davies was the beneficiary of a superb surgical operation in 1953 which re-built a shoulder he had smashed on a concrete surround while touring in Romania. This fine full back's career thus had two phases – pre–1953, when he won four caps with Swansea, and post–1957 when he was a Stradey Park regular, played for Wales seventeen more times, and finished up as skipper.

Norman Gale was one of the most effective hookers ever to play for his country, but his improbable talent as a place-kicker is not to be overlooked. As skipper of Wales against the 1967 All Blacks he ran out of patience as, one after another, his specialist kickers let him down with missed penalty chances. Finally Gale himself planted the ball down at thirty yards' range and hoisted his kick neatly between the posts. He kicked another pressure goal at Cardiff in a rare victory by Llanelli in 1967.

Gale, yet another product of the great Gowerton Grammar School nursery in the west, won twenty-five caps, a total which puts him third in the list of Llanelli's International players.

Delme Thomas toured New Zealand with the 1966 Lions before being capped for Wales, and his forty-four appearances for the British Isles are the most by a Welshman. Though not the tallest of men at six feet three inches, he nevertheless was a world-beater in the line out during the early 'seventies.

A key member of the Llanelli side which beat New Zealand in 1972 was the powerful centre **Raymond Gravell** – and it is hard to imagine a greater partisan. 'Grav' is the archetypal Scarlet, one for whom 'my club, right or wrong' is life's credo. He even admits to founder-membership of the notorious 'Cyclops' club of ultra-committed Llanelli supporters.

In his early years Gravell was a master of the outside break, adding bulk and a ferocious hand-off to powerful acceleration. In later years Wales, for whom he played twenty-three times, used him in a crash-ball role, at which he was very effective. But many prefer to remember the way he played at the outset of his career. In retirement he brings the same passion to his work on radio and TV which characterised his displays on the field.

John ('J.J.') Williams was the most important of the three key players who came to Stradey Park from other clubs in 1972 (Chico Hopkins of Maesteg and Tom David from Pontypridd were the others). Lured partly, no doubt, by the glamorous prospect of participating in Llanelli's Centenary season with its fixture against New Zealand, and partly by the chance of learning from the club's then coach Carwyn James, Williams moved from Bridgend to give his adopted club great service in a stay that lasted until December 1980 with 205 appearances and 159 tries. His thirty appearances for Wales, with twelve tries, make him Llanelli's most capped player. He went on two Lions tours, scoring twelve tries for McBride's team of 1974 in South Africa.

Williams, an International sprinter, was a beautifully balanced runner who appeared to cover the ground effortlessly, gliding outside opponents and always able to find an extra yard of acceleration. He also mastered the art of the controlled chip over defenders' heads.

Late in the 'eighties he became involved in improving Welsh International teams' fitness – the crucial nature of which was brought grimly home during the 1988 tour of New Zealand.

NEATH RFC

HQ: The Gnoll
Strip: Black

Behind all top clubs there functions a cadre of dedicated workers who attend to the marshalling of playing strength, coaching, ground and accommodation requirements, fixtures, travel and the attracting of support and members. But a side which lifts itself away from a week-to-week routine existence to a level where

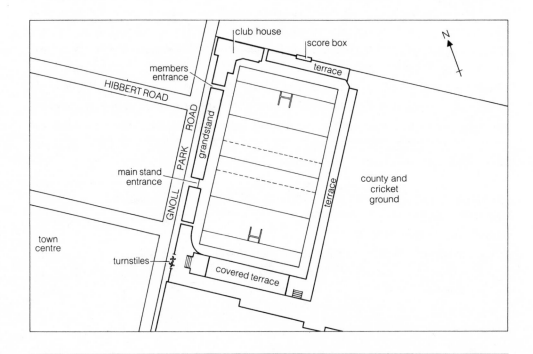

match play is something special and titles are won usually owes its success to the key influence of a single person. For much of the nineteen eighties Neath RFC had such a man.

After becoming the first club to win the modern Cup competition, later known as the Schweppes Cup, the Welsh 'All Blacks' meandered along Rugby Football's middle lane for more than a decade. Their performances were never bad, they could always pose a threat to opponents, and they produced players of calibre. But there was little consistency in their approach. No trophies came their way. Administratively they appeared short of ideas. A sniff of stagnation hung over The Gnoll.

In 1982, however, they surprised their critics by having the imagination to appoint the Welsh game's first-ever team manager. A product of the local grammar school, and a Cambridge Blue, Brian Thomas had won twenty-one caps as a lock forward between 1963 and 1969. He continued in club Rugby for a few more years (appearing in the 1971 Cup Final) before stepping into the wings to concentrate on his career with the British Steel Corporation. He emerged in 1982 with a broad-based role covering selection and player liaison, plus the declared intention of restoring Neath to their rightful place among the elite group of Welsh clubs.

He did that. In six years his men swarmed their way back to the top with stylish, effective Rugby that brought them Championship and Merit table titles, plus three appearances in Schweppes Cup Finals. The club supplied a crop of players to the National XV, some of them quite outstanding. Scouting and talent-spotting initiatives were intensified, ensuring a constant in-flow of high-quality youngsters. Spectators returned to throng The Gnoll's touchlines and crowd its stands. Membership boomed.

Business pressures – he was now self-employed – brought about Thomas's abrupt resignation in November 1988. Though his burning desire to bring the Cup back to Neath had remained unfulfilled he undoubtedly re-ignited the club's desire for success – with a blend of massive dignity and earthy entreaty. Eschewing comfortable seats among the VIPs on match days, he preferred to stalk touchlines from which he could encourage – or berate – his players. A giant of a man, he was someone they looked up to in all senses of the word. They probably feared him, too. But they certainly played for him; and in return he instilled in them a sense of pride in achievement that had been absent from the Gnoll before the Thomas era.

It was natural that when the Welsh Rugby Union came to be founded in 1881 Neath should be chosen as venue for the formal drawing-up of documents. Premier club representatives met together at the town's Castle Hotel, a short distance from Cadoxton Field. Here, a decade before, local youngsters first let off steam with the help of an oval ball and rules imported from public schools in England which they were sent away to attend. Their games led to the foundation of Wales's first major Rugby club.

The leading light in these early gatherings was a Scot, T.P. Whittington, who had played for his country against England in 1873. In all likelihood it was he who decreed the all black strip which his club adopted then and have stuck with ever since. A player called Moxham turned up one day wearing a cap emblazoned with a small Maltese cross, which team-mates decided would look good as an adornment to their somewhat dour jerseys. By 1898 the club were installed close to the town centre at premises named after the nearby Gnoll House, home of a country gentleman.

Neath's influence on the game continued to be important. It is claimed that in 1888 E.V. Pegge pioneered the wearing of shorts, as opposed to breeches (though there are counter-claims on behalf of the Maori tourists who came to Britain that year). But about Walter Rees's pre-eminence there can be no argument. He became secretary of the Welsh Rugby Union in 1896 and remained in office for an astonishing forty-two years.

The All Blacks were always front-runners in the unofficial Championship campaigns between the wars and immediately afterwards, winning titles in 1911, 1929 and 1947. This was the period when the club built a reputation for iron-hard forward play, with great men like Glyn Stephens, Tom Arthur and Arthur Lemon to the fore. But behind them danced backs like the extraordinary Dan Jones who scored what is thought to be a world record seventy-three tries in one season: fifty-nine for his club, two in Welsh Trials, six for Glamorgan and a further six in a Great Western Railway International match. Neath's forward tradition was extended in the 'forties and 'fifties through Rees Stephens, son of Glyn, line out ace Roy John and the magnificent prop forward Courtenay Meredith who won total respect from the tough South African scrummagers of his era.

The club touched another peak in the late 'sixties and early 'seventies. In those days the heroes were Brian Thomas, Dai Morris and the Welsh-bred Scotsman Wilson Lauder. Polished full back Graham Hodgson lent steadiness to a back division full of ideas and penetration which saw the All Blacks through to a Championship title and the successful Cup Final appearance of 1972 when the favourites, Llanelli, were toppled. Dai Parker, at five feet two inches one of the smallest men ever to have played first class Rugby, scored the winning try.

Under Brian Thomas's management in the 'eighties, Neath added a fresh dimension to the tradition of tough, closely concentrated forward play. Now they fielded packs which moved swiftly around the pitch, getting to the breakdown and driving on or releasing possession to three quarters who were orchestrated by Jonathan Davies during four brilliant seasons. Paul Thorburn emerged as a top-flight full back, and his dynamic entries into the line were finished assuredly by 'Inter City' Elgan Rees, Alan Edmunds and Graham Davies. Among Thomas's attributes was the capacity to attract and mould distant talent which might otherwise have found its way into other clubs: Kevin Phillips, Rowland Phillips and Jeremy Pugh, all from the Welsh heartland, were captures who demonstrated the team manager's pulling power and the long spread of his scouting tentacles, as was Cornishman Colin Laity. From nearer at hand Mark Jones and Stuart Evans were irresistibly drawn to the bandwagon rolling along at the Gnoll.

Immediately on Thomas's resignation, Neath named Ron Waldron as his successor. A formidable front row forward, whose career climaxed in the Triple Crown year of 1965, Waldron linked with Glen Ball on Neath's coaching strength after a period with nearby junior club Resolven. It was a hard act that he elected to follow, but his predecessor made it clear that he would remain on committee and be available as an elder statesmen.

The general appearance of The Gnoll has altered little in recent years, but slowly and perceptibly the club has been improving and modernising its facilities. Progress has been made with the provision of smart, comfortable reception rooms above the main clubhouse block. A large cash outlay funded the re-furbishment of somewhat gloomy changing accommodation for players and referees. There has been the construction of an ample steel deck above the grandstand for television cameras, which for long had to shoot into the rays of a setting sun from temporary platforms above the popular bank. The bank itself, serving as a vantage point above both the Rugby pitch and the adjacent cricket field (where W. G. Grace once bagged a 'pair'), could do with new, more elevated terracing for the benefit of the big crowds which flock to cheer Neath's flamboyant style.

Pressmen, too, would welcome more agreeable accommodation. Neath committeemen grew tired of having their legs pulled with calls for the switching on of the electric bulbs which cast a dim glow on the hacks' notes on December afternoons, and up-graded the illumination; but increased elbow room, better desks and more telephones would be a good idea.

Such innovations are well within the reach of a club which, though cautious by nature, is well run and stands proudly in the front rank of world Rugby. The

Roman legionaries who founded Nidum would have approved of the gladiatorial combats staged in today's Vale of Neath.

Great Days at the Gnoll – and Elsewhere

19.12.1912: Neath 3pts, South Africa 8pts

Considering their seniority in Welsh Rugby, the failure to be awarded fixtures against the 1888 Maoris, the First New Zealand All Blacks and the First Springboks must have been a bitter pill for Neath to swallow. The 'golden quartet' of Cardiff, Llanelli, Newport and Swansea all met the big Dominions' touring sides and founded reputations as high-fliers of the Welsh scene.

So the men of the Gnoll clearly had points to prove when they met the Second Springboks under Billy Millar. The outcome, not well refereed by a Mr Miles from Leicester, was one of the most tempestuous afternoons of the century. The crowd bayed its disapproval at the tourists' first try which followed a cross kick at which the scorer, 'Boy' Morkel, appeared offside.

Having been unable to convert Otto van der Hoff's earlier try, Duggie Morkel now added two points to give South Africa an interval lead which was soon eroded by Handel Richards's interception and unconverted try for Neath. But amid mounting tension Mr Miles disallowed scoring bids for the home side by Tom Lloyd (knock-on) and Will Hopkins ('no apparent reason' said the Welshman) – and maybe deserved the clod of earth hurled at him near the close.

In 1919 Neath went down 10–3 to the New Zealand Army XV, but thereafter for many seasons it was their fate to be harnessed uncomfortably with Aberavon in games that never allowed them, or their partners, to give of their best.

6.5.1972: Neath 15pts, Llanelli 9pts

Cup competition in Wales had been in abeyance since 1914 when constant brawling disfigured the Final and persuaded administrators that knock-out tournaments were not compatible with the Welsh attitude to Rugby – among players and spectators.

Its restoration, therefore, in 1971–72 was an act of faith on the part of the WRU. Their reward was an excellent series crowned by an eye-catching Final watched by 12,000 people. It was Neath's triumph to win the Cup in their Centenary season.

They were not the favourites, having lost three times to their opponents in Championship fixtures during the previous six months. Motivation, however, was with the All Blacks on the big day, with tearaway flanker Mike Thomas frustrating the young Phil Bennett's efforts to swing the game Llanelli's way. Burly John Poole kicked three penalties to match the Scarlets' penalty goal and penalty try converted by Andy Hill, and tiny David Parker squeezed past opposing full back Roger Davies to claim the decisive score.

Afterwards Martyn Davies and his men established an enjoyable tradition by trotting round Cardiff Arms Park on a lap of honour before repairing to the changing rooms and waiting champagne.

28.4.1984: Neath 19pts, Cardiff 24pts

Once again Neath found themselves with an underdog rating for the Schweppes Cup Final, though this time they could not deny Cardiff a third victory in four years.

But they captured the glory, outscoring their opponents by three tries to two and succumbing only to the precise goal-kicking of Gareth Davies – who was otherwise ruthlessly policed by the tireless open-side flanker Lyn Jones. However, the personal triumph of the day belonged to the plucky little miner Gareth Jones. At just twenty years of age, he showed no signs of match nerves and set the formidable Terry Holmes, his opposite number, all kinds of problems. During the first half he intercepted a pass and raced eighty metres up the south touchline at the National Ground to be floored at the flag by a desperate Gerald Cordle cover tackle, before bouncing back to score from the set scrummage. His tenacious all-round display secured him the Lloyd Lewis Memorial Trophy presented by the Welsh Rugby Writers to the Man of the Match, an unusual award to a member of the losing team.

6.5.1989: Neath 14pts, Llanelli 13pts

Before a near-capacity crowd at Cardiff Arms Park for the second year running Neath's all-out attacking style, evolved under Brian Thomas and polished by Ron Waldron and Glen Ball, at last bore fruit. Llanelli fought for the full eighty minutes to hold onto the Schweppes Cup, but the Blacks were in no mood to be swept aside as they had been twelve months previously.

Tries by Mark Jones (who also spent a deserved ten minutes in the sin-bin for stamping and could not have complained at a sending-off), Brian Williams and finally

Paul Williams – with a Thorburn conversion) crowned an outstanding season for the men of the Gnoll. They set a world record of 1917 points which included no fewer than 345 tries. Kevin Phillips emerged as an inspiring, if at times impetuous, skipper and pack leader.

Heroes of the Gnoll

Glyn Stephens had set high standards for Neath in the pre-1914 era, but it took a further decade before two worthy successors emerged at The Gnoll to pick up his mantle and cement Neath's reputation for powerful forward play. **Tom Arthur** was born at Pontypridd, but police duties took him west and he won the first of his eighteen caps in 1927. Arthur's versatility leaps out of the bald statistics: besides being able to play in all three rows of the pack he was an accomplished heavyweight boxer.

Arthur Lemon was a back row specialist who came into the Welsh XV at the end of the lack-lustre 'twenties. By the time he joined St Helens Rugby League club in 1933, Wales had found a new lease of life and were on an upward curve that was to last for twenty years. Successively a tinplate worker and policeman, Lemon's finest hour was his display at Swansea in 1932 when his destruction of the English midfield brought a first victory in the fixture for Wales in ten years.

After the Hitler War, Neath packs enjoyed another decade of dominance, with a pack built around **Rees Stephens**, a worthy son of his father. This bustling lock, who loved to play with stockings round his ankles, was a vital component in the powerhouse of tight play who yet managed to move rapidly around the field and could play in the back row. The winner of thirty-two caps, he captained his club for three seasons.

Stephens's own fame is shaded by his long-lasting partnership with **Roy John**. A potent club combination, the pair also appeared ten times together for Wales.

Just as David Marques and Robert Norster would do in later years, John ruled the line out during the 'fifties. Though not the tallest of men, he soared above the opposition and brought down possession in two large hands to be delivered in mint condition to the scrum half. John's presence helped Wales to two Grand Slams, he was in the 1951 side narrowly beaten by South Africa, and he figured in the 1953 team which beat the All Blacks.

Courtenay Meredith, too, was on duty for Wales that day, a prop who won fourteen caps. This steelworks official brought both physical power and technical expertise to his role, and the Welsh eight were seldom out-scrummaged in his time.

The immense behind-the-scenes contribution of **Brian Thomas** at the Gnoll has been noted, but his days on the field were memorable too. Besides pushing his full weight at set pieces he was expert in the mauls, using considerable upper-body strength to rip possession clear. His twenty-one International caps were supplemented by three Cambridge Blues and two seasons as captain of his club.

And as Thomas was bowing out, another all-time great Neath forward was establishing a presence in the Welsh pack. **David Morris**, known to all and sundry and Max Boyce as Dai, came into representative Rugby as a number eight, figuring in Wales's high scoring 1967 defeat of England before switching to flanker for the remainder of his thirty-four caps. Not for nothing did he earn the nickname 'Shadow', which may have owed its origins to Gareth Edwards whose breaks he so often supported. Lean of frame, Morris covered the open field with a loose, rangy stride but was equally at home in the hurly-burly of tight play.

Graham Hodgson won fifteen caps as a full back in the traditional last-line-of-defence mould, but his substantial achievements were eclipsed in the 'eighties by auburn-haired **Paul Thorburn**. After showing consistently imaginative club form, the University College, Swansea, graduate forced his way into the Welsh side in 1985 and a year later won a unique place in Rugby history with the longest penalty goal ever kicked at Cardiff Arms Park. Measured at seventy yards, eight and a half inches, it contributed massively to Wales's 22–15 win over Scotland. By the end of that International season Thorburn had run up a record fifty-two Championship points in four games.

Despite clinching Wales's third place in the 1987 World Cup with a touchline conversion that just pipped Australia in the play-off, Thorburn found difficulty in making his International position secure. At the outset of 1989, however, his strong leadership capability was recognised with the captaincy of his country as Wales began their Five Nations Championship bid.

NEWPORT RFC

HQ: Rodney Parade
Strip: Black and amber

The top Welsh clubs vie with each other to claim the best records and achievements, providing impeccable facts and figures to support their respective cases. But few rolls of honour are as lengthy or glittering as that of Newport.

For a start they can point to no fewer than six unbeaten seasons. Only two other

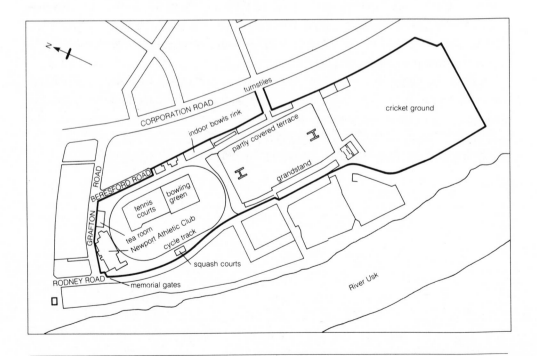

Welsh clubs, Swansea and Maesteg, have gone through a campaign without defeat, and then only once each.

The other great measure of calibre in Wales is performance against major touring sides. Newport are the only club to have beaten South Africa twice. They took the Wallabies' scalp in 1957 and were responsible for the solitary defeat inflicted on Wilson Whineray's fine All Blacks of 1963. And, when all other clubs in Wales crumbled before the mighty 'Kiwis' of 1945–46, Newport held them to a 3–3 draw. Such feats speak for themselves; but it is hard to resist including the spicy statistic recorded by club historian Jack Davis in his volume *A Hundred Years of Newport Rugby*: for a club game against Bristol, Newport once put out a team of fifteen Internationals from Wales, England, Scotland and Ireland – and had three capped players in reserve.

Nor would Newport want one special and unique distinction omitted – that of belonging both to the Welsh Rugby Union and to the Rugby Football Union.

The majority of these distinctions, however, came the club's way a long time ago. In recent years the Black and Ambers have drifted along, seemingly becalmed on the edge of Rugby's mainstream. During the nineteen eighties the players supplied to the National XV could be counted on the fingers of one hand (though they do include the ebullient Mike Watkins, briefly a smiling skipper of Wales). No major 15-a-side titles have come their way. The traditional stream of Gwent Valleys players that used to pour Newport's way has, it seems, dried up. With the exception of hosting the annual Snelling Seven-a-Side Rugby tournament, modern Black and Amber supporters find it hard to point to any radical development or major innovation beside the Usk. On the contrary there has been an occasional regression to bully-boy tactics: some players have got themselves involved in unpleasant, unsightly punch-ups and scuffles (as on the occasion of the 1985 Fijians' visit); others have had to be severely disciplined for sending-off offences, and on one occasion a referee turned his back on a brawling game involving Newport and left the pitch to them and their opponents. Such incidents, combined with sudden unexplained defections by key players, are usually the sign that a club has temporarily lost sight of its aims and values.

Even Rodney Parade itself, for long a name that has resounded magically within world Rugby's corridors of power, scarcely stands up to close scrutiny as a venue for big Rugby. On my bookshelves is an ancient coaching manual written by Gwyn Nicholls, the great centre three quarter of this century's first decade; some of its illustrations depict play at Newport – with, in the background, the same popular terrace with the self-same overhead cover.

The club are aware of the ground's shortcomings. They know that changing-room facilities desperately need up-grading. The two-hundred yard walk from the clubhouse to the Rugby pitch is an ordeal players should not have to undergo at any time, certainly not between December and February. Spectator accommodation, both terrace and grandstand, is less than luxurious. Medical and toilet provision close to the field of play must be improved. The visitor does not get the impression that his presence is being courted.

Newport's Rugby men do not like washing their dirty linen in public. However, their sport, though arguably the one bringing in cash and prestige, is just one of no fewer than ten Sections which constitute the Newport Athletic Club. Outsiders cannot help but be aware of the tensions and dissent that trouble Rodney Parade from time to time and would appear to have affected initiative. Arguments about how funds should be divided and disagreement about priorities have certainly impeded development.

Now, however, the five-acre cricket ground at the arena's south westerly end (a gift from Lord Tredegar in 1892) has been sold to Gwent County Council, the club is about one million pounds better off, and a tremendous chance is at hand to make progress. There is nothing like a big cash injection to breed a mood of confidence, and at last the Rugby stadium can anticipate its long-promised overhaul with players' changing rooms being moved to a convenient position beneath the grandstand. Offices, bars and reception rooms will be smartened up. It is likely that the indoor bowls hall, at present somewhat constricted, will be expanded in order that extra rinks can be laid down and international events hosted.

It will be surprising if Newport RFC do not sweep into the next century on very buoyant spirits indeed.

A relatively unlovely Victorian town founded to export coal and iron, latterly the centre of a contracting (but now stable) steel industry, Newport has got its second wind as a place of importance. The scars of smokestack industry are being expunged, new hi-tech factories abound, and the mouth of the River Usk is about to be plugged with a barrage. That implies a constant high tide, which will cover forever the unsightly mud-banks from which bedsteads and bicycle frames jut here and there. A better prospect thus awaits those heading for Rodney Parade, the majority of whom must cross the town bridges by train, car or foot – though they may wonder with slight unease what will be the dam's effect on playing conditions. The local saying is that, if the tide is out, the pitch is springy and agreeable; if it is in, then it will be at its soggiest and heaviest. Some of that million pounds may need to be spent on improved drainage.

There are plenty of quiet and noisy corners for a pre-match pint at Rodney Parade, but on an autumn or spring afternoon many spectators like to foregather outside the headquarters buildings where the Newport team and their opponents arrive to change. They stand chatting on the fringe of the steeply-banked cycle track which was built in 1892 and until three decades ago staged a multitude of important meetings – now, alas, it is used mainly for car parking. The foreground view takes in courts which play host to international and championship tennis; the modern George Street suspension bridge is an elegant backdrop, and the Rugby stadium occupies the middle distance with its grandstand. Opposite the grandstand is the covered terrace from which matches are televised and from which vantage point club official and former International Brian Jones broadcasts match commentaries to hospitals in Gwent.

As kick off time draws near, folk move off to watch the action. This has in recent years been of an uneven quality. The Tony Faulkner coaching period, which occupied much of the 'eighties, produced excellent packs crammed with strong, dour forwards in the characteristic Gwent mould, which enabled his sides to compete with the best teams in the world. What went down well at Pontypool, however, was not enough for a club with Newport's broader concept of Rugby football. Backs could be forgiven for feeling like second-class citizens (and indeed looked like them at times), flair and imagination appeared to evaporate, and spectators voted with their feet: the great stadium was as often as not less than half full. Sadness was felt by friends who had applauded Newport's great days and the play of men like Ken Jones, Roy Burnett and the two Watkinses, Stuart and David.

Now, as has been noted, there are strong reasons for believing that better times lie ahead. But for them to happen on the Rugby field itself, as well as on the perimeter, the breeze of change which introduced new coaching personalities and new attitudes in 1988 must be allowed to blow the dust away. Doors and windows must be opened to let the fresh air in.

Great clubs are amenable to such imperatives. That is what differentiates them from the rest. And despite occasional periods of muted performance, Newport belong in their number.

*

Seven-a-side Rugby football has never exercised the same hold over the Welsh as it has in England and especially Scotland. That it has achieved respectability and a certain frivolous respect is largely due to Newport. In 1951 representatives of sixteen top clubs under the chairmanship of Newport's Bill Everson persuaded the

WRU to legitimise a seven-a-side tournament which was held for the first time at the end of the 1953–54 season. The then chairman of Newport RFC, R.S. Snelling, gave the splendid trophy.

The tournament peaked in popularity during the 'sixties when it regularly filled the old Cardiff Arms Park. Then several factors dented its appeal. A succession of cold Mays came along, with people unable to laze in the sun swigging beer and munching pork pies while watching sunshine Rugby. Increasing tour pressures prompted top players to make themselves unavailable. Coincidentally, new Laws made the 15-a-side game better to watch. Thus in recent years the 'Snellings' has tended to travel along rather aimlessly. It began life at Rodney Parade, and currently is back there with Newport RFC striving gallantly to re-vitalise it as a pre-season spectacular.

Newport themselves have won the tournament ten times.

Newport's Greatest Days

30.10.1963: Newport 3pts, New Zealand 0pts

Wilson Whineray's Fifth All Blacks were undoubtedly cast in the classic New Zealand mould. The captain ranks with his country's best leaders. Men like Meads, Tremain, Gray, Waka Nathan and Don Clarke are among the finest ever in their positions. When the time came to fly home the tourists could claim not only a reputation as splendid entertainers but also a record showing only one reverse in thirty-six games.

That defeat was administered at Rodney Parade and is probably the finest of all Newport's magnificent accomplishments.

Though the New Zealanders were having only their third match of the tour it should not be imagined that they were rusty. They had run up over fifty points in brushing aside Oxford University and Southern Counties, and were firm favourites as they took the field in drizzling rain before 25,000 spectators.

The game was never going to be a spectacular one. Newport had decided on a defensive policy involving do-or-die tackling and the killing of rucks to deny the All Blacks second phase possession. Throughout the game Glyn Davidge was the 'fall-guy' who put this policy into action, though it is more than doubtful that he would have got away with such tactics under today's Laws. As it was, the siege-gun kicker Don Clarke did not get one penalty attempt at goal throughout the match.

The New Zealand back row were given constant cause for concern by half backs Bob Prosser and David Watkins, and it was a fast outside break by the latter which brought the afternoon's only score. Stuart Watkins received and put in an intelligent cross-kick; John Uzzell gained possession and dropped a smart goal that just cleared the crossbar from twenty five yards. The moment is captured in an oil painting hung in Newport's clubhouse.

The All Blacks were matched thrust for thrust until late in the game when they unleashed a series of frantic assaults. Newport held on grimly to complete their trio of victories over Dominion touring sides.

12.11.1969: Newport 11pts, South Africa 6pts

The Black and Ambers rang down the 'sixties with a resounding win over the demonstration-wracked Sixth Springboks. Given the political unacceptability of South Africa in world sport the feat enabled them to set a record which may stand for ever – that of twice defeating the Springboks, the first victory having taken place in 1912.

Despite being the reigning club champions, Newport were not favourites on this day. Their erstwhile skipper Brian Price had retired, phenomenal young Keith Jarrett had turned professional and the International number eight forward John Jeffery had been forced to withdraw through injury.

In the event the result was seldom in doubt, partly thanks to the Springboks' missed penalty chances, partly thanks to inspired leadership from John Anthony. Though never capped, the full back was a class player with all-round skills who had been quick to embrace the Australian 'dispensation' experiment which encouraged running out of defence. He was instrumental in creating his team's second try, also contributing a conversion and a forty-yard penalty. South Africa could reply only with penalty goals.

17.2.1951: Cardiff 3pts, Newport 8pts

Though a low scoring match, for those who saw it, this clash between Newport and their age-old rivals was unforgettable – not just because of the second-half hailstorm which saw players huddling on the ground or hiding behind goalposts for protection.

This was the third meeting of the clubs in 1950–51 (in the old days they played each other four times a season). Newport had enjoyed a magnificent run of thirty-three successive victories, and the prospect of a do-or-die attempt by

Cardiff to end it drew 48,500 people to Cardiff Arms Park. The attendance remained a world record for a club fixture until overtaken by the 56,000 who saw the 1988 Schweppes Cup Final. In retrospect it certainly marks the zenith of 'friendly' club Rugby as a spectator sport.

Playing into a stiff breeze the visitors conceded a first half penalty goal kicked from long range by Ewart Tamplin. But ten minutes after the break they asserted themselves when Doug Ackerman, now the club secretary, and Bob Evans broke away to put Tom Sterry in for an equalising try. Now Newport were not to be denied and after a Ken Jones thrust which panicked the Cardiff defence, Bryn Williams picked up a loose ball and sent John Lane flying over for a try which Ben Edwards converted.

Newport's winning run lasted another month. It ended with a controversial 3–0 defeat at the hands of Harlequins whose touch-judge afterwards admitted to having raised his flag in error, thus preventing an equalising score.

30.4.1977: Newport 16pts, Cardiff 15pts

Few performances against Cardiff can have given Newport as much satisfaction as their 1977 Schweppes Cup Final win which deprived their opponents of the trophy they dearly desired to crown their Centenary season.

The pack, in which veteran Ian Barnard played the game of his life to be voted 'man of the match' by the Press, shaded that of Cardiff, while an outstanding contribution was that of young Chris Webber at centre. Always dangerous with the ball in his hands, he also contributed the superb touchline conversion of Jeff Cranton's try which effectively put his side just beyond the reach of Cardiff's late rally.

This game was the first of two successive appearances in the Final in which Newport's progress was plotted by John Ryan who became Wales's coach in 1988. They failed to win the Cup a second time, however, going down narrowly to Swansea.

22.10.1985: Newport 38pts, Barbarians 29pts

To ease pressure on the famous Barbarian club's Easter tour, Newport agreed to sacrifice their traditional Tuesday fixture in exchange for an autumn date. Beginning in 1982 the new arrangement has seemed to satisfy everyone, not least the Rodney Parade regulars, who have consistently been treated to uninhibited, open Rugby and heavy scoring.

Above: Haydn Tanner was in two winning sides over the Third All Blacks. In 1945, however, his Swansea XV went down to defeat at the hands of the 'Kiwis'

Right: Three fine Welsh forwards in action against the 1953 All Blacks. Rees Stephens (Neath) is at left; Billy 'Stoker' Williams challenges in the foreground, with skipper John Gwilliam just visible above his head

Above: Clive Rowlands: 'Kick me the salt, dad'!

Left: David Watkins: crowds flocked to marvel at his speed off the mark

Above left: Carwyn
James wearing a
British Isles
tracksuit in 1971:
the outstanding
British coach of the
twentieth century

Above right: Barry
John ... 'could
ghost through
defences'. Fergus
Slattery of Ireland is
left clutching at
straws

Right: John Dawes:
a gifted centre with
great tactical
insight – and a great
captain of the
British Isles

Eyes riveted to the target area, Gareth Edwards is about to swing the ball beyond Natal defenders' reach in 1974. The man from Gwaun cae Gurwen is acknowledged as the finest scrum half to represent his country

Terry Holmes: a tiger on the field

It is hard to imagine a more exciting player than Gerald Davies. But here he is trapped by two Irish defenders at Cardiff in 1973

J. P. R. Williams: 'surging into the three quarter line'

Below: Robert Jones: there is no telling how he may blossom given a constant supply of good ball

Right: With the ball, Billy James, one of the great men of Aberavon

Left: Mark Ring: a centre with genuine penetrative powers and originality

Below: Pontypool's great pack was the platform for their 1983 Schweppes Cup triumph. Here David Bishop prepares to exploit perfect possession against Swansea

Above left: Gwyn Evans: an elegant player who could turn in an expert performance anywhere in the back division

Above right: A pained look on the face of Swansea's Dick Moriarty. Had he been allowed to specialise in one position he could have become one of the truly great Welsh forwards

Right: Bleddyn Bowen looks for space as he leads Wales to victory over Scotland in 1988

Above left: Steve Fenwick, with thirty caps Wales's most-capped centre

Above right: At the outset of 1989 Paul Thorburn's strong leadership capability was recognised with the captaincy of his country

Left: Despite not having the licence enjoyed by predecessors Jonathan Davies often created opportunities for match-winning tries

Probably the most thrilling of these evening games so far was that of 1985 when both sides threw caution to the winds and opted for all-out attack. Twelve tries were snapped up, two of them by the Black and Ambers' live-wire flanker Richie Collins, later to be capped from South Wales Police. The lead changed hands a breath-taking eight times before Newport pulled away to win.

The following year, it ought to be recorded, the Barbarians took grim revenge, winning by fifty points to seventeen.

Newport's Heroes

Arthur Gould, who won twenty-seven caps between 1885 and 1897 heads Newport's roll of honour. In the nineteen fifties and 'sixties old timers who had watched all the twentieth century stars still considered him the greatest of all. Wrote 'Dromio', one-time critic of the *South Wales Argus*, 'No three quarter I have known maintained the high level of attainment in attack and defence so long and so consistently as Arthur Gould – no man has shown such uniform brilliance and resourcefulness over so long a period of years.'

Jack Wetter was skipper in Newport's last unbeaten season, that of 1922–23 when the club ran up 462 points from thirty-nine games, with points against just 112. A fine tactical controller, he won ten caps in a variety of positions behind the scrum. He was a double International who also played baseball for Wales.

The two **Travers, George**, the father, and **W.H. 'Bunner'**, his son, were Wales's hookers for ten seasons between 1900 and 1949. They were a super-tough family, who are supposed to have invented a diabolical training ruse at their nursery club, Pill Harriers in the early years of the century: young forwards being trained to deliver their whole weight at the scrummage had to push with their backs to the coke oven which heated the changing room. Giving ground meant severely scorched flesh!

'Bunner' was one of the select band of Internationals who appeared for their countries before and after World War II. He picked up four caps as late as 1949, and few people could credit that this was the same man who had first hooked for Wales in 1937.

R.T. 'Bob' Evans was among the best of a long line of powerful forwards who came to Newport from Gwent's small northern townships. Born in Rhymney, he was just nineteen in 1939 and the World War undoubtedly robbed him of a stack of caps in the back row. A policeman, he captained the 1946 Monmouthshire XV which beat the Kiwis and Wales could not wait to blood him in the unofficial 'Victory' Internationals of 1946.

He made an important contribution to the Grand Slam of 1950, subsequently touring Australasia with the British Lions.

The centre **Malcolm Thomas** is perhaps one of the least feted but certainly most consistent of Newport's great men. A long-striding runner who could break all but the strongest tackles, he won twenty-seven caps and skippered his club to the Championship in 1956. In his National service days he was the youngest captain ever of the Royal Navy XV.

Thomas had one most unusual distinction. As a Lion in 1950 he was the baby of the side; on his second trip in 1959 he was the oldest member.

Stand off half **Roy Burnett** was a streak of black and amber lightning. Spindly legs produced acceleration that left defenders for dead. It was his misfortune to be a contemporary of Wales's sitting tenant Cliff Morgan, and he won just one cap.

His thirty-four appearances between 1954 and 1962 make **Bryn Meredith** Wales's most capped hooker. A superb technician, he was also a lithe and speedy athlete who covered the field like a back row forward.

His Rugby upbringing took place at West Mon school, Pontypool, a great cradle of the game, and subsequently at that centre of athletic excellence, St Luke's College, now absorbed into the University of Exeter. Meredith went on two Lions visits to South Africa including the 1955 tour with its drawn Test series.

Brian Jones is the only living player to have been on winning sides against touring XVs from each of the major southern hemisphere nations: Newport's teams against the 1957 Wallabies and the 1963 New Zealanders and the Barbarians XV against the 1961 Springboks.

A thrustful centre who was unlucky not to add to his two caps of 1960, Jones subsequently devoted his spare time to the administration of Rugby at Newport, whose chairman he was in their Centenary year, and for the Merit Table group of clubs, whose secretary he became in 1987.

Peter Rees was a determined runner with the ball who won four caps for Wales between 1961 and 1964, when he toured South Africa with Wales.

Brian Price led Newport in his third season with the club, captained Wales to a Triple Crown in his final season and was one of the best line out jumpers the game has seen. In recent years his pointed, often whimsical, contributions on club and International matches have become a feature on BBC radio.

Though his twenty-six caps were won in an era that was less than lustrous for his country, **Stuart Watkins** still managed to collect nine tries for Wales, including a magnificent effort which denied France victory at Cardiff in 1966. Intercepting a loose pass on the Welsh twenty-five line, the wing set off into the teeth of a gale, swerving and handing off with great guile to keep defenders at arm's length and finally flop down exhausted at the corner flag after a pulsating run.

Once into his stride Watkins was hard to pull down. Newport benefited from his scoring power, which helped him amass 345 points for the club, all in tries.

Michael Watkins was a dogged skipper of Newport and Wales when both club and country were experiencing hard times. He could and did raise a smile on beaten teams' faces when necessary with some extrovert humour and mimicry, but this may have taken more out of him than was generally realised and his retirements from both the representative and club games were abrupt.

Besides being a fine hooker 'Spike' was expert at burrowing into mauls and emerging with the ball.

PONTYPOOL RFC

HQ: Pontypool Park
Strip: Red, black and white hoops

Anyone imagining that the South Wales Valleys are bleak, dismal places should watch Rugby football at Pontypool Park in the spring or autumn. The steep, wooded hillside rising over the eastern side of the town is ablaze with colour: bronze, red and flame tinted in the first half of the season, brilliantly green in March and April. It is a sight to cheer the soul.

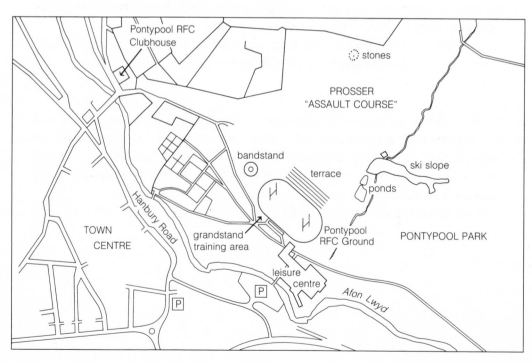

Torfaen Borough Council have not been slow to exploit the site's possibilities. Beside the bank of the fast-flowing Afon Llwyd stands Pontypool's Leisure Centre which once won commendation as the best of its kind in Britain. The nearby parkland has walks and a bandstand. Above it an artificial ski-slope snakes through the trees – as does the 'assault course' which toughens the muscles and sinews of players who represent Pontypool on the Rugby pitch at its foot.

This is a magnificent arena for sport, though there may have been little opportunity to dwell on its charms for opposing sides who have been put through the mincer there in the 'seventies and 'eighties. For during these decades Pontypool have been the most consistently daunting hosts in Britain, throwing down before visitors a grim gauntlet backed up by a mailed fist. Occasionally supremely gifted or determined opponents have managed to depart with the spoils, raising eyebrows in the Rugby world; but victories have been the habit for the home team, roared on by a tumult of sound pouring from the popular bank and the small, trim grandstand: 'Poola! Poola! Poola!'

In this long heyday, the club has enjoyed tremendous support bordering on the fanatical, drawn from the whole of the valley and beyond. Had it owned its own ground it could probably have doubled or trebled its season ticket sales by extending the seated accommodation, but this is something upon which the Council, as landlords, have yet to embark. Nevertheless, the tenancy is one which suits Pontypool RFC: the annual rental that they pay hardly breaks the bank, and allows them complete freedom to train, play and take gate money. Since the Park is open, there is no means of ensuring that every spectator seeking a vantage point on the hillside pays entry money; but officials believe that for the most part their fans pay up with a grin to watch a club that has taken over from Newport as Gwent's top attraction.

As everyone must know, the supremacy that Pontypool for long enjoyed was based on a succession of magnificent forwards, their efforts brought to the boil by the inimitable Ray Prosser. The well-known names tumble quickly into print: Cobner, Perkins, Squire, Butler, Staff Jones, Brown, Faulkner, Windsor and Price – the three last-named forming the original Pontypool Front Row. And beside the capped players there packed down a supporting cast of supremely able club forwards like Steve Jones, Mike Harrington and Chris 'the Madman' Huish. Behind-hand, for several seasons, there were try-scoring wings in Goff Davies and Bleddyn Taylor and a fine tactical controller in Mike Goldsworthy. When pressure play compelled opponents to concede penalties, the admirable Dr Peter Lewis would step up from full back to kick goals.

The other key player of the 'eighties was scrum half David Bishop who came as near as any back could to stealing the Pontypool forwards' thunder. His 1986–87 season was flawed by controversy and an eleven-month ban imposed by the Welsh Rugby Union, and his club faltered. Then, the following winter, Bishop was joined at half back by the gifted Mark Ring who was discontented with the selectorial policy at his native Cardiff club. The pair revelled in the acres of space put at their disposal by the pack, and steered their team effortlessly back to the top. Pontypool smiled contentedly; a new dawn was evidently at hand.

Alas. The 1987–88 season looks in retrospect no more than a glorious Indian summer.

By September 1988 Ring had patched up his argument with Cardiff and gone back to the Arms Park. Bishop had cashed in his chips and gone north. Senior forwards opted for retirement or jobs with the media. Without Lewis, the kicking of decisive goals was no longer a formality.

Pontypool began to stumble and stagger, and almost overnight forfeited the on-field respect that had been accorded to them by a whole generation of opponents. There was an early-season thrashing at the hands of Bath, soon followed by sixty-point defeat at Stradey Park. To top up their winter of discontent an administrative oversight led to their dismissal from the lucrative Schweppes Cup competition for fielding an ineligible player in their 10–9 win over junior club Vardre.

The club had been hit by a swing of the pendulum which affects all participants in Rugby football as the years go by. They had rarely been able to produce or attract International-calibre backs, and now the famine was dire. Worse, the conveyor-belt of robust, adaptable forwards who had fitted into Prosser's packs like square pegs into square holes ceased to function. Cheerful new coach John Perkins kept a brave face, but the proud club were taking colossal blows to their self-esteem and morale was harder to sustain than it had been for years.

There seems no doubt that Pontypool will get their act back together in time. Men of great determination hold the helm including Terry Vaux, club President and a Wales member of the International Board, Bob Jeremiah (who is shortly due to break Rowley Meredith's record as secretary, with nearly a quarter of a century's service), and Ray Prosser himself as team manager. As they chew food for thought, however, it may well occur to them that for long their side has been like a dinosaur, an enormously powerful animal with magnificent physique and muscles – but a small brain.

That is, it could crush ruthlessly anything which moved less quickly than itself and which it could catch. Under Cobner and Butler, Pontypool packs moved around the pitch like an all-enveloping red, white and black blanket. They scrummaged menacingly low, driving opponents back – and then back again – with a concerted snap-shove. Their loose play was innovative; notably the 'rolling maul', which was pioneered at Pontypool Park, could often advance play fifty or sixty metres upfield and for a time was almost unstoppable. Their rucking was clear-cut and directed at moving over the ball; occasionally opponents would be shifted out of the pack's path with insteps or shins – but the difference between this and kicking or stamping was the same as that between a hand-off and a punch.

Such supreme forward skills, however, frequently seemed to be employed for their own sake; and having completed a manoeuvre that brought roars of appreciation from the sidelines, Poola would do it all over again rather than release possession for the backs to sweep past a disorganised defence. Three points from a penalty, rather than four or six from a try, seemed a sufficient, unambitious reward to their impassive forwards as they trotted back to the half way line (though it is only fair to add that, when given ball, wings like Goff Davies and Bleddyn Taylor could strike unerringly).

The second great failing was an inability to change gear or style in response to a nimble, quick-witted challenge. Thus when Cardiff, Llanelli, Neath or a Wallaby touring side arrived to play a crunch Cup or tour match, Pontypool's response could be one of puzzlement and mystification at the strange twist the game was taking. There was an inability to lift their approach from its week-in, week-out level of robust efficiency. So, although their displays over the whole of the season's eight-month campaign were regularly outstanding, in these long, golden years they won the Schweppes Cup just once. In a word, they could not peak.

Nevertheless, their achievements between 1970 and 1988 – the Prosser years – were unparalleled. This former lock, who moved up to prop in Welsh or Lions packs, lifted his club from a lowly position in the Rugby hierarchy to its summit. They won the Whitbread title six times, the Western Mail unofficial Championship five. In 1973 and 1975 they finished top of both tables, and their Cup triumph took place in 1983. They passed the 1000-point mark for a season on twelve occasions, and set a world record of 1607 in 1983–84.

Eleven forwards and one back were capped by Wales, six of these men also touring with the British Isles; and a further six gained B caps. Back in the 'seventies it was Pontypool who provided the forward core of a series of magnificent Welsh International teams, granting the same space to Edwards, Bennett and Gerald Davies that was created at Pontypool Park.

Such distinction is mirrored in the clubhouse. Its trophy room sparkles with silver cups and bowls, International caps, and portraits of the great – not to mention clay caricatures from John Hughes's 'grogg shop' over at Pontypridd. Reception rooms on match day are full to overflowing with camp followers of a mighty tradition. Conversation is enthusiastic, articulate and informed. The place amounts to a great repository of Rugby lore, a bubbling think-tank that will sustain and stimulate John Perkins and his coaching colleagues as they seek to plot a way back to the top. Perhaps what is wanted is vision – of the kind that Bishop and Ring briefly and brilliantly bestowed: the capacity to see beyond the heels of the back row.

And lest anyone should doubt that Pontypool have a heart of gold, consider, finally, the case of Roger Addison. This promising young forward broke his neck in a match at Rugby in 1966, since when he has lain paralysed and immobile in Cardiff's Rookwood Hospital. For two decades he has been able to do little for himself beyond operating the delicate mechanism that changes channels on the TV screen suspended from the ceiling.

Throughout this period Pontypool have taken care of his few creature needs with unfailing loyalty. Catastrophe struck their man down in his prime; yet with constant visits to his bedside they demonstrate the camaraderie and fellow-feeling of the Rugby game. This, as well as success on the field, is true greatness.

Great Days at Pontypool Park

1.1.1927: Pontypool 6pts, New Zealand Maoris 5pts
8.12.1927: Pontypool 6pts, New South Wales Waratahs 3pts

It would be wrong to imagine that Pontypool's only golden era was in the 'seventies and 'eighties. Although not formally founded until 1901, the club rose to take the unofficial Championship in 1913–14. In the immediate post-war years their pack acquired the nickname 'terrible eight', with quick-striking hooker Cecil Pritchard in the van. This period in their history was crowned in 1927 by a unique 'double' in the same year over two major touring sides.

The Second Maoris were their first opponents from overseas. They came with victories over France, Cardiff (twice), Newport, Yorkshire and Lancashire under their belts, only to be unsettled by Pontypool's tremendous forward commitment. The home side took the lead when a long pass reached auburn-haired wing Cliff Richards who tore in for an unconverted try near the corner. A second-half try by centre Ira Thomas put them just out of reach, though wing Falwasser replied for the tourists with a try converted by Potaka – his second kick, after Pontypool charged too soon.

In the final ten minutes the Gwent side's defence proved heroic, with full back Cliff Ford bringing off match-saving tackles. The result was a second defeat for the New Zealanders to cap that suffered at Stradey Park.

The Waratahs who provided the opposition at the end of the year boasted an even better record than the Maoris. They could point to six victories in Wales, including the scalps of Llanelli and the Welsh National XV at Cardiff.

Pontypool, however, continued where they had left off in January with a full-blooded forward effort which gained them a pressure penalty goal kicked by Frank Beddington. A flowing three quarter move initiated by stand off Tom Lawton and carried on by centres Egan and Wallace brought an equalising try for the tourists scored by W.H. Mann. But Pontypool responded to the urgings of 20,000 spectators with a final offensive which broke the stalemate and yielded a winning try for powerful centre Don Cormack.

30.4.1983: Pontypool 18pts, Swansea 6pts

Though the capture of the Schweppes Cup was a triumph for well-drilled Pontypool, the crucial encounter had really come at Cardiff two months earlier. The previous four Cup meetings between the clubs, all at Pontypool Park, had ended with Cardiff victories but now, in the Fourth Round, penalty goals by Peter Lewis and a John Perkins try were too much for their bogey opponents. After a semi-final win over Bridgend, Jeff Squire's men arrived at the National Ground on a high.

A disjointed Swansea side failed to deliver the expected challenge and Pontypool's pack blazed the victory trail in what was described as a low-key match before 37,000 spectators. But at least Pontypool could say they did it their way, with Mark Brown and Squire outstanding up front and Bishop controlling events from scrum half with a huge variety of tactical kicks. Four penalty goals by Peter Lewis and his conversion of a single try by Bleddyn Taylor were enough to see them through.

1987–88: The Greatest Season

When Bridgend won at Pontypool Park in September 1987 most people thought another ordinary season was in store for the home side. Instead the statistics show thirty-five massive victories, with just the Cup semi-final defeat by Neath as a second blot on the copybook. This was awesome consistency.

With John Perkins now team coach, the great pack which had sustained the club in the 'eighties enjoyed a long final fling under Steve Jones. For Ring and Bishop it was an *annus mirabilis*, the former supplying 357 points, the latter scoring thirty-five tries. Their understanding was instant, their entertainment value unsurpassed.

Pontypool did notable doubles over Llanelli and Neath, and won three times against Cardiff – home, away and in the Cup. Maesteg conceded sixty points, and South Wales Police lost twice by 53–13 and 52–13. The final points tally was 1011 for, 411 against.

Heroes of Pontypool Park

At the outset of their history Pontypool had an outstanding family of **Jones** boys, **D.P.**, **Jack** and **Tuan**, whose efforts put the young club on its feet. Rugby historian J.B.G. Thomas names J.P. as the best of the three, 'a centre who could be ranked with R.T. Gabe and Gwyn Nicholls'. J.P. won fourteen caps and toured with the British Isles in Australasia and South Africa.

In 1913–14, a mere thirteen years since their formation, Pontypool won the Welsh Championship with only seven defeats in forty-four matches. In this era, miner **Bob Lloyd** was the outstanding back, a scrum half who won seven caps in the years leading up to the outbreak of war before turning professional.

It was tempting to bracket **Thomas Raymond – Ray – Prosser** along with the other Welsh International superstars. Instead he belongs here, as the quintessential clubman – one who, it is said, became homesick the moment the team bus travelled south of Croesyceiliog.

He appeared over three hundred times for his club, mostly as a lock forward, moving up to the National XV as a prop in 1956 following the retirement of Courtenay Meredith and Billy Williams. He finished in 1961 with twenty-two caps.

But it was during his Lions tour to New Zealand in 1959 that 'Pross' had his eyes opened to the major possibilities of power forward play as practised by the All

Blacks. For a while after hanging up his boots he watched and studied Pontypool at play from the popular bank; and at last, in 1969, began the eighteen-year stint in which he put his carefully conceived theories into practice. He worked on every movement, every posture, every stride that had a bearing on forward play; he taught individual skills; and then he welded players' abilities into a unit. His packs became the most accomplished ever seen in Wales.

And finally, he was a supreme motivator. His men took the pitch prepared to die for Pontypool – and their coach. His pre-match pep-talks may never find their way into the National Library of Wales (and were certainly unsuitable for children's ears). But he was a master of the kind of rhetoric which has a place in the changing rooms of Rugby Football.

Schoolmaster **Terry Cobner** was Prosser's lieutenant on the field of play, skippering Pontypool during most of the nineteen seventies. A loose forward with a devastating tackle, he was fast around the field and possessed good hands. But Cobner also revelled in the tight exchanges where his eight would gradually and inexorably grind the will to resist out of opponents. All in all he was a very complete forward.

He also had the leadership qualities required in a good captain, as the British Lions found in 1977 when he fired up the tourists' forward effort to the level where it could offer the All Blacks a serious challenge.

'We may go down; we may go up; but we never go back,' was the grim credo of the Pontypool Front Row which jointly represented club, country and – once – the British Lions in the latter part of the 'seventies. **Bobby Windsor**, its senior member, was a fast-striking hooker who could also deliver his full weight at set pieces. During many of his thirty-three International appearances (five for the Lions) he could be counted on as a second pack leader, able to infect team-mates with his own uniquely abrasive approach to the forward battle.

Ageless **Tony Faulkner**, known for most of his playing career as 'Charlie', was a loosehead prop whose power and technical correctness put people in mind of Prosser himself. A Black Belt at judo, he gave best to no man at the heart of mauls and scrummages. Although he is not remembered for great deeds in open play, one of Rugby football's most memorable photographs depicts 'Charlie's' delighted, toothless gallop over Ireland's line for a try in his first International season at Cardiff in 1975.

That was the year when the PFR first appeared together for Wales, **Graham Price** making up the trio. Though in one sense he is inseparable from his fellows, his forty-one caps – the most won by a forward for Wales – mean that he appears in the constellation of Welsh stars discussed elsewhere.

The other great influence on modern forward play at Pontypool was **Jeff Squire**. A loose-limbed giant of a man, he could play equally well at number eight or on the blind side and acquitted himself well on Lions tours against the powerful packs of the southern hemisphere. A product of Newbridge Grammar School who moved up the first-class ladder via St Luke's College and Newport, he became a Welsh selector in 1988.

Like his great predecessor as Pontypool's coach, **John Perkins** learned much from a short sojourn in New Zealand early in his career as a lock forward. His bulk and technical expertise won him recognition in the Wales B side of 1977, but he had a long wait before his first full cap came along in 1983. This was the first of eighteen appearances for Wales, when he was a model of consistency.

Cambridge Blue **Eddie Butler** was cast in the mould of the great Pontypool forwards and led his men intelligently and with élan. At International level he found himself in charge of Welsh teams which lacked the greatness of the previous decade and carried the can for the slow decline which set in during the 'eighties. However, he did know how to handle **David Bishop**, a stormy petrel who arguably stole more headlines than any other Rugby player in this period. Acknowledged by many as the most gifted athlete-player of his generation, he possessed skills of the very highest order and was exactly the right kind of scrum half to exploit the opportunities created by Pontypool's assured forward play. A short fuse meant that he was often in hot water, on the field and off it, and he never won the wholehearted trust of the Welsh selectors, who awarded him only one cap.

The fact remains that for seven seasons, until he turned professional with Hull Kingston Rovers in July 1988, Bishop was a supreme crowd-puller, idolised at Pontypool Park.

SWANSEA C&FC

HQ: St Helen's
Strip: White, black stockings

To speak of Swansea RFC, sticklers in the west rightly insist, is a malapropism: the full name is Swansea Cricket and Football Club. It was founded, they will explain, in 1872 to play soccer, enthusiasm for which evaporated after only two matches. Having turned to the handling code for their winter exercise, members

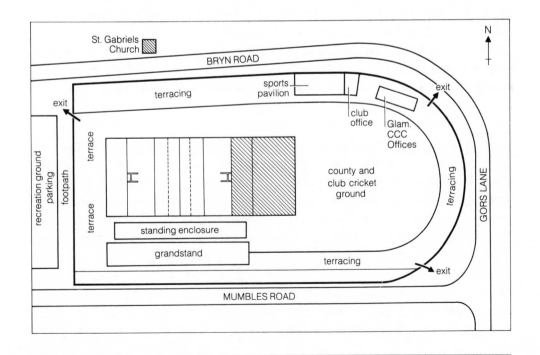

voted to amalgamate with the local cricket club to give themselves something to do in the summer. And it is a quirk that, although the Rugby club's tradition and achievements can bear comparison with any in the world, its St Helen's headquarters is best remembered by the world at large for a cricket record.

Here it was, during a match between Glamorgan and the touring West Indies, that Garfield Sobers unleashed a unique assault on the Welsh county's stock bowler Malcolm Nash, lashing him for an unprecedented six sixes in an over. A junior television cameraman happened to be under tuition while the main crew took a tea-break, so that fortuitously the feat was recorded for posterity along with Wilfred Wooller's commentary rising to its near-apoplectic crescendo. Every so often on nostalgic occasions it is re-screened – to the chagrin of Malcolm Nash.

But Swansea has been the scene of momentous events in Rugby football too. It was at the local Tenby Hotel in 1880 that sixteen clubs sat around a conference table to found the Welsh Rugby Union. Not surprisingly in consequence, St Helen's staged the first home International match played by Wales, in 1883. Australia were beaten by Swansea in 1908, South Africa in 1912. And, on a crowning day of days in 1935, the All Whites became the first club team to beat New Zealand. Haydn Tanner and Willie Davies were the schoolboys who helped dash the Third All Blacks to an 11–3 defeat.

Ireland completed a Triple Crown Championship campaign at St Helen's in 1949 with a 5–0 win over Wales and Swansea achieved a 6–6 draw with the Fourth All Blacks in 1953, but since those days nothing quite so dramatic has taken place in the Rugby enclosure. Nevertheless Swansea have regularly managed to serve up entertainment of high quality; and when they have been absent, their ground, as a neutral venue, has staged some stirring Schweppes Cup semi-final ties.

There is ample car-parking space at St Helen's, but for anyone who has time, the walk from the city centre is an agreeable one, with ozone and a view of Mumbles Head all the way. The Maritime Quarter, where you can eat lunch in one of the new hostelries overlooking the yacht marina, makes a good starting point. At its western end stands West Glamorgan Council's striking new headquarters, while away to the right rise the local gaol, the grandstand at Swansea City AFC's Vetch Field and the angular tower of the Guildhall (well worth a call to see the magnificent murals by Sir Frank Brangwyn which dominate its assembly hall). Swansea Bay curves along on the left, the Uplands form a landward backdrop, the quaint little Patti pavilion named after the legendary soprano of the turn of the century stands in its garden surrounds, and the nearby Cricketers Arms (where one of Sobers's sixes fell to earth) is well positioned for a pre-match pint.

The £120,000 floodlights that dominate the twin-purpose stadium are of a high enough quality for Glamorgan to have staged a 'pyjama game' beneath them in August 1988. Batsmen agreed that the orange ball could be picked up easily, a point proved by Javed Miandad and Dean Jones who struck a series of massive blows towards the stars. However, these same lights misbehaved on one notorious evening when Swansea were entertaining the 1984 Wallabies. With fourteen minutes of play left and the tourists 17–7 ahead a 400-amp fuse blew, plunging the stadium into darkness and forcing the abandonment of the game. At least the home team's blushes were spared that night.

Perched on rising ground to the west, the clubhouse offers a commanding view of the playing area from its noisy, friendly main bar. The building itself is roomy and comfortable, if in need of a coat of paint here and there – which is why the club launched a £100,000 Appeal in 1988 to fund a major renovation programme.

There is a limit, however, to what Swansea C and FC can achieve at St Helen's, since the lease of the ground was surrendered to the local Council in 1943. The latter's attitude to the Rugby club's requirements has been positive to the point of generosity; witness its speedy response when the Safety of Sports Grounds Act enjoined re-structuring of the grandstand and enclosure. But the magnanimity of a landlord is no substitute for the liberty of action enjoyed by a freeholder. There must be times when the club's committee feel frustration that, for instance, they cannot take advantage of the space beneath the stand to upgrade their existing facilities and provide extra amenity rooms.

The capacity of the stadium is a moot point since theoretically the terracing could be packed on three sides as it was in 1953 when 45,000 saw Swansea's game against the Fourth All Blacks. Since then the pitch has been moved west, however, and the club has ensured a good view for spectators at its eastern end by installing temporary seating for matches against major touring sides. A realistic figure today, therefore, would be 30,000, most of whom would be accommodated on the big popular bank which slopes diagonally away from the Rugby pitch.

This last feature is one that can fox even the greatest of players. Half backs often use the alignment of a crowd along a touchline to calculate the correct angle for a split-second tactical or clearing kick; but on the north side of the St Helen's pitch this is an unreliable guide. Another hazard is the prevailing south-westerly wind that can unbalance a match and spoil the enjoyment of the players and spectators by weighting the advantage heavily in favour of the team playing with the elements.

But the great glory of this ground is its pitch. So often in midwinter the dismal story from the rest of Wales and the United Kingdom is of frostbound or waterlogged turf. No such circumstances have had to be endured by George Clements of the twinkling eyes and fondness for a glass of stout or Richard Stevens, who has succeeded him as groundsman. Salt air checks the frost, the sand in the topsoil makes for instant drainage – and St Helen's is unplayable once in a blue moon.

What is more, its hard but springy surface encourages players to run and handle. Low scores at Swansea are rare.

The character of Swansea C&FC certainly includes an eagerness to pioneer and innovate. It was the first western club to tour behind the Iron Curtain in the early 'fifties, playing Romania in Bucharest before an estimated 90,000 spectators. Their hosts paid a return visit to Wales in 1955 which launched them on a trail which was to see them seeded in the first World Cup of 1987 with the game's senior nations. 'Swansea,' telegraphed the President of the Romanian Rugby Federation on the occasion of the club's Centenary in 1974, 'represents for our people a symbol of Rugby football at the highest level.'

The 'Whites' were also quick to embrace the coaching ideal and took on strength the former Llanelli coach Ieuan Evans at the start of the 1970 season. A club publication contains his admirable advice on blending the contribution of star players with the more pedestrian efforts of the rank and file: 'A team's highly gifted members, a rare species, must always be conscious of their dependence on their fellow players. The converse is also true in that the supporting cast must be aware of the significance of . . . providing the necessary platforms from which individual artistes can launch their own particular brand of wizardry. There is no rivalry, ill-feeling or jealousy in a well-integrated team, for this divisive trinity will destroy a Three Musketeers atmosphere.'

Evans later became a Vice President of the Welsh Rugby Union, wrote a major report on the state of the game in Wales (which has not seen much daylight) and became chairman of the WRU coaching committee. At Swansea his successors were the gifted Stan Addicott and former hooker Jeffrey Herdman.

Swansea's latest controversial decision took great boldness, flying in the face of their peer clubs who make up the Whitbread Welsh Merit Table group. Confronted with the WRU's determination to graft a league competition onto the traditional fixture system, the Whitbread clubs voiced vigorous opposition for numerous reasons. Swansea begged to differ, and declared in favour of leagues – given common-sense provisos, for example, that there should be thorough consultation on matters of organisation and finance.

How would Swansea fare under a league system? Would they win titles? Would they be a middle-of-the-table-team? Or is there a danger that they would suffer the humiliation of relegation?

The great paradox of Swansea is the club's failure consistently to deliver the goods in terms of titles and Cups. Their one and only Schweppes Cup success was as long ago as 1978 (they have lost three Finals in the 'eighties). Once only have they headed the Whitbread table, and they can point to only one title in the forty years since World War II in the *Western Mail* newspaper's unofficial Championship series. This despite being blessed with galaxies of talent and regularly supplying key players to the Welsh national XV.

Could it be that an element in Swansea's character rejects the pursuit of success for success's sake? Their style does not feature the blazing passion of Llanelli, Pontypool's single-mindedness or Cardiff's poise and composure.

They neither gloat over victory nor brood on defeat. Theirs is the smiling face of Rugby; they are cavaliers in the game.

Swansea's Greatest Days

26.12.1912: Swansea 3pts, South Africa 0pts

Swansea's best results are now sunk deep in the dusk of history, yet from many decades' distance they can still reflect gleams of glory. The trio of victories over the 1908 Wallabies, the 1935 All Blacks and, in between, the Second Springboks mean that up until the Second World War, the All Whites stood out as the world's most famous and feared club side.

The notorious prevailing wind which gusts straight off Mumbles Head down the St Helen's pitch played its part on the famous day when, in front of 35,000 spectators, Bill Millar's South Africans fell to defeat. It assisted the home team to carry the battle to heavier opponents and pin them deep in their own half. For once, too, the playing surface was waterlogged, which set the tourists extra problems. Swansea knew just what tactics were needed, and after twenty minutes a fierce foot rush drove the ball over the opposition line where prop D.J. Thomas snapped the decisive try.

The heroics came in the second half, as the South Africans threw in everything they had. Stegmann, McHardy and Luyt were robbed of tries by tremendous covering and tackling. As the visiting forwards tried to develop foot rushes, Swansea fell bravely to make loose balls safe. For a while fourteen defenders had perforce to do the work of fifteen while wing Howell Lewis received attention on the sidelines. But the Springboks could not produce an equalising score, the normally dependable Doug Morkel missing with four penalty attempts.

Since injury had kept key men Jack Bancroft and Rev Alban Davies out of Swansea's ranks, the success must be counted as a triumph of leadership for Billy Trew, one of the greatest of all backs and the winner of twenty-nine caps between 1900 and 1913.

28.9.1935: Swansea 11pts, New Zealand 3pts

Perhaps this was the greatest result of all for a Welsh club.

New Zealand's All Blacks had acquired an aura of invulnerability, having lost only one match (to Wales) out of sixty-five played in 1905, 1924 and the first weeks of their 1935 visit. Swansea, on the other hand, had lost their last four games against touring sides, had no top-flight players with the exception of Claude Davey, and had selected two schoolboys at half back, the Gowerton Grammar School cousins Haydn Tanner and Willie Davies.

The latter two stole the headlines after the club's victory. From the reports, however, it is clear that the All Whites' pack under Edgar Long chose the occasion for a super-charged display which provided the artful young halves with time and space for indulging their genius. Another crucial factor was the steadying presence of the vastly experienced Davey at centre, crash tackling in devastating form and running in two of his side's three tries.

But the young half backs' influence was undeniable. Tanner alarmed the tourists' back row with early sorties that nearly brought tries and tied them in for most of the game; Davies tormented their midfield with inward jinks and outside breaks. 'Don't tell them back home that a couple of schoolboys beat us,' tour skipper Jack Manchester begged Pressmen afterwards.

12.12.1953: Swansea 6pts, New Zealand 6pts

A third Swansea teenager bobbed up in 1953 to deny New Zealand the spoils at St Helen's. This was the strapping John Faull who turned the scales at 15 stones at the tender age of nineteen. Best remembered as a back row forward, on this day he was at centre where his crash-tackling was in the best Claude Davey tradition.

More important, he placed the two long-range penalties with which Swansea drew the match.

For New Zealand Alan Elsom ran in two tries, but though Bob Scott and Ron Jarden peppered the posts with conversion attempts, drop kicks and penalties no winning score came.

26.11.1966: Swansea 9pts, Australia 8pts

Critics are fond of saying that the Fourth Wallabies were not up to much. Certainly the loss of their captain John Thornett early in the tour was a disturbing factor. The fact is, however, that they won two of their Tests in the United Kingdom, beating England 23–11 and a confident Welsh XV 14–11. Swansea's narrow victory, by a try, a dropped goal and a penalty to a goal and a try thus appears in a strong light.

The match, however, was disfigured by constant brawling among the packs. Afterwards the Australians criticised what they called the indecisive refereeing.

29.4.1978: Swansea 13pts, Newport 9pts

Their Cup Final victory, in which a capable Newport side had the will to resist squeezed out of them, seemed to have set Swansea on course for a golden era. A brilliant crop of youngsters under Alun Meredith included David Richards, Alun Donovan and Richard Moriarty who were to achieve great things on the International field. Alas, they have so far failed to repeat their Schweppes triumph.

The Black and Ambers tenaciously declined to throw in the towel, a hat-trick of penalties by Chris Webber keeping them in contention right to the final whistle. It has to be said, however, that they rarely threatened their opponents' line, being forced to play much of the game on or near their own 22-line from which Richards and Gareth Jenkins dropped goals and Roger Blyth put over a penalty.

The Cup was won by a smart piece of opportunism on the part of a pair of Swansea front row forwards. International prop Phil Llewellyn won brisk short-line possession near the Newport corner flag, where stocky hooker Jeff Herdman surprised the defence with a ten-metre dash for an unconverted try.

Swansea played three Finals in the 'eighties, losing on each occasion.

St Helen's Heroes

A century ago **Jack Bancroft** was the 'name player' who pulled in fans everywhere to watch his daring exploits. First picked by Swansea as an eighteen-year-old in 1889, he scored over 1000 points in a career that lasted well into the twentieth century. He made thirty-three consecutive appearances at full back for Wales and was in his country's first-ever Triple Crown winning team of 1893 when he coolly placed a winning dropped goal.

Bancroft's favourite trick was taunting tired forwards by running them to and fro across the field before driving them back with huge clearances to touch.

Billy Trew was something special. Wrote the great critic of the *South Wales Argus*, Dromio: 'Name whom you will for knowledge of the game, individual skill, the ability to inspire or fit into a scheme of combination; praise whom you may for the power to give the best and educe the best – and there is no-one to place above Trew for unobtrusive skill and unfailing judgement.'

The 'twenties were not a vintage period for Wales, but **Rowe Harding** managed to leave a significant mark on the game with seventeen caps and five International tries. A Blue and a Barbarian, this speedy wing also toured South Africa in 1924. In later life he became a respected circuit judge, and accepted the Presidency of his club.

W.O. Williams's twenty-two caps as a prop forward were won between 1951 and 1956, his career peaking on the famous Lions tour of 1955 when the Springbok forwards were tamed at the scrummage.

Before his time few demands had been made of Welsh tight forwards away from the set pieces. To the traditional brawn of the steelworker, however, 'Stoker' added the new skills of rucking and mauling which were now required by the front five.

Dewi Bebb was one of a small but select band of north Welshmen who have broken the south's monopoly on International representation. Experience at Trinity College Carmarthen, Cardiff Training College, the Royal Marines and United Services Portsmouth meant that when he joined Swansea he was already a very complete player. The Welsh selectors agreed and gave him the first of his thirty-four caps against England on 1959. On a horrendously muddy day Bebb squeezed over in the corner for the game's only try.

This product of Friars School, Bangor, was a deceptive runner. He could often make progress despite an apparent lack of space, but was careful to cultivate a kick-and-chase technique to employ when he was finally cornered. He had a dependable pair of hands.

Geoff Wheel sweated and toiled his way to a total of thirty-two caps in the 'seventies and was a cornerstone of a great Welsh side. Though a fine scrummager, he reserved his most important contribution for the maul: in the midst of the turmoil his blond head of hair would be seen bobbing and jerking – until finally the ball was presented, on a plate, to his scrum half.

After the departure from International Rugby of Phil Bennett, **David Richards** was hailed as one who would automatically step into his boots. Despite winning seventeen caps in a five-season career, however, the slim, dark-haired midfield player never became a fixture in the National XV. Gareth Davies was the stand off preferred by the Welsh selectors, and in the end Richards even surrendered his number ten club jersey to play his last season or two as a centre.

His running was always brimful of excitement, and the four International tries he scored were gems. His confidence was troubled, perhaps, by an inability to raise his line kicking to the standard of precision required at representative level. In 1987 he was a welcome recruit to Wales's selection panel.

Richard Moriarty's contribution to Swansea's recent history has been considerable – and could have been even greater.

In his early seasons this strapping forward was often in hot water on the field and off it, only to mature into a sensible and responsible skipper of his club. The captaincy of Wales followed, and though Moriarty suffered agonies as his team crashed 49–6 to New Zealand in the World Cup, he had the consolation of leading them in the 22–21 win over Australia in the third-place play-off.

He was used, or perhaps exploited, by club and country as a lock, number eight and blind side flanker. Many critics believe that had he been given the chance to specialise in one of these positions he could have become a truly outstanding forward.

Robert Jones won twelve schoolboy caps and appeared for the All Whites while still a sixth former at Cwmtawe Comprehensive School. He moved into senior Rugby as Wales's scrum half at Twickenham in 1986, quickly becoming a fixture despite a strong challenge from Llanelli's Jonathan Griffiths, and by the close of the 1989 season had piled up twenty-six caps – though still just twenty-three years of age.

Influenced by All Black Dave Loveridge at an early stage in his career, Jones developed a short, snappy pass in the modern mould which won him plaudits during the 1987 World Cup. To date, many of his International appearances have been made behind packs struggling to hold their own, and there is no telling how he may blossom with a constant supply of good ball.

A GLAMORGAN
QUARTET

GLAMORGAN WANDERERS RFC

HQ: The Memorial Ground, Ely
Strip: Cambridge blue, black and white hoops

Years ago, before their Ely era began, Glamorgan Wanderers' headquarters were in fourth-floor premises above one of Cardiff's elegant Victorian arcades. Here the club's numerous fifteens and their opponents retired after matches to chat, gossip,

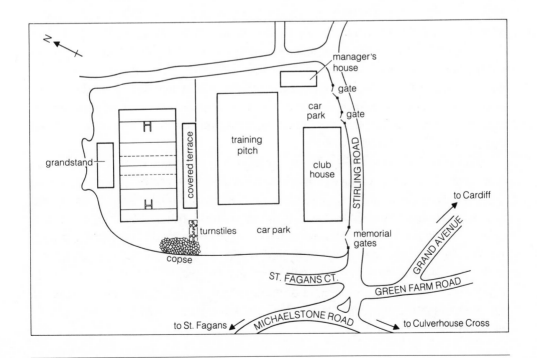

argue, drink and sing the evening away. Local Pressmen, as honorary members, were often present to add spice to the exchanges.

The bar and lounges were reached on board an ancient lift which squeaked and groaned at the human tonnage it was required to bear aloft. As far as I can remember it was the sole means of entry and, more significant, egress; and the problem of an escape route in case of fire must have exercised the minds of many visitors. There was talk of a flight path that threaded its way between the chimneys and across adjacent roofs to descend near the old-established Costa Rica Coffee Company or (better still) Brain's Brewery; but mercifully it was never required.

The Wyndham Arcade 'den' was the club's sixth base. Founded by a group of old boys from Cardiff's Monkton House private school, who wished to perpetuate their teenage Rugby camaraderie, they began with matches beside the River Taff at Sophia Gardens field, property of the Third Marquess of Bute. There followed days near the Claude Hotel in Roath, the Bishop's Field under the shadow of Llandaff Cathedral, the Fox Field at Whitchurch and the Common nearby. When the membership base was broadened in the twentieth century and a new name was called for, it is not surprising that the choice fell upon Glamorgan 'Wanderers'. The Rugby football boom in the nineteen forties helped to set them on a sound financial basis and an Appeal to members resulted in the raising of enough cash to buy a meadow in rural surroundings at Ely, which was named the 'Memorial Ground' after the many players who had lost their lives in two world wars. The club were able to spend some £8000 – a small fortune in those days – on laying out pitches and building a tiny but attractive grandstand. Today the original lay-out has been augmented by a covered terrace on the southern side, which was opened with due panache by entertainer Max Boyce in the autumn of 1987. Nearby, a capacious clubhouse complex has sprung up and become the nerve centre of a vital and purposeful Rugby football operation.

Because of their origins, the Wanderers' image for much of their history has been that of a happy-go-lucky, moderately well-to-do grouping with a strong upper-middle-class membership: 'that most English of Welsh clubs' it was called by J.B.G. Thomas. And if there is a watershed on the other side of which travel, jerseys, meals and a certain amount of free beer become 'perks' taken for granted, the Wanderers have generally remained on its scarp slope as true amateurs, paying for their Rugby with annual subscriptions and match fees. They have rarely had money to burn, and the couple of fixtures that they were allowed to stage in the 'twenties at Cardiff Arms Park, which yielded a 'gate', were very important to their coffers.

But since they purchased it, the Memorial Ground has been inexorably ringed around with new housing, as Cardiff's western suburb of Ely swelled to giant proportions. A recently-built spur of the M4 runs a few hundred yards from the dead-ball area, facilitating teams departing on their Wanderings and making access straightforward for visitors.

The Wanderers' character has changed to take account of such factors, one of the most important being the potential for support and new playing blood in the growing neighbourhood. One sign of the times came in 1976 when, after long agonising in committee, it was decided to install turnstiles at the Memorial Ground. This also reflects the quality of new fixtures the club have secured with the advance in their playing record. As members of the Whitbread Merit Table, in which their best achievement so far has been to reach the runners-up position, they now compete with all Wales's premier clubs (they beat Cardiff and Llanelli in the 1982–83 season) as well as Bristol and Moseley. They have also won the Snelling seven-a-side trophy.

Success breeds success and the Wanderers can claim to have groomed some of the best club players to emerge in the 'eighties: the ability of Pat Daniels, Nick Ward, Andrew Yeandle and Andy Martin bears witness to expert tuition and nurturing. But the new problem which arose was the departure to more 'fashionable' sides of key players whose expertise had guaranteed success in specific aspects of match play. For instance, when Owain Williams left in 1987 to join Bridgend and link up with brother Gareth his erstwhile team-mates were deprived of a sure source of line out possession from which many rapid-fire manoeuvres were developed. To hold such men, in the words of former club coach Gerald Williams, the Wanderers need another good campaign in the Merit Table or the Schweppes Cup, preferably culminating in the winning of a major trophy. It looked as if such targets might be achieved in 1987–88, a season which the Wanderers began with an unbeaten run of seventeen games. Dismissal from the Cup at Tredegar in controversial circumstances, however, disturbed their rhythm, so that ultimately their playing record was no more than adequate.

Gerald Williams was himself a good example of a short-term factor that can work in favour of a suburban side like the Wanderers and plug gaps. He came to the club in the evening of his career and stayed on after retirement to mould the Wanderers' first team fortunes. There was pleasure, too, in 1987 when Mike Goldsworthy returned to the fold after a highly successful period as Pontypool's stand off half. And in October 1988 Robert Lakin, a resolute and experienced Cardiff back row forward for ten seasons, also made the move to the Memorial Ground. The arrival of such men both strengthens a team and adds to its stature in the eyes of youngsters viewing the first-class scene and calculating where their best future may lie.

There is a theory that economic buoyancy has an effect on confidence and energy which goes far beyond industry and commerce. If that is the case, Glamorgan Wanderers will take heart from the boom which the city of Cardiff is now experiencing. They are already on an upward curve and are among the best-equipped clubs to make an impact on twenty-first century Rugby.

Great Days at the Memorial Ground

23.8.1986: Glamorgan Wands. VII 30pts, Cardiff VII 6pts

Though the scene was Rodney Parade, Newport, the 1986 Snelling Sevens final was certainly Glamorgan Wanderers' finest hour. They took the title for the first time, administering upon Cardiff their heaviest defeat since the competition began in 1954.

Despite a 43–0 defeat in the previous year's final, the Wanderers had won recognition as an up-and-coming sevens force. They went true to form in 1986, first beating off a tremendous challenge from Aberavon who led them by two points into injury time before succumbing 16–10. They also conceded twelve quick points to Swansea before recovering; but in the final there were no such hiccups: Cardiff were denied possession by a rampant Wanderers VII who, though deprived by injury of skipper Geoff Wyatt's input, ran in six spanking tries. Nick Ward won the Bill Everson Award as the tournament's outstanding player.

28.10.1987: Glamorgan Wanderers 25pts, USA Eagles 6pts

The Memorial Ground was packed for the Wanderers' first fixture against a major touring side and the home team duly swept to a victory which suitably commemorated the occasion. The game itself, however, was less than entertaining, with the Americans unable to match their opponents' skills at scrummage and line out. Their stand off Mark Williams kicked for position, and in the first half Mike Goldsworthy did likewise for the home team.

Once Paul Prickett and his men realised that the tourists presented no real threat they took control and rucked them off the park. Steve Best and Ian Hemburrow scored tries, goal-kicker Brian Bolderson building up the impressive winning score-line with three penalty goals and two conversions.

MAESTEG RFC

HQ: The Old Parish Ground
Strip: Black and amber hoops

It is now just over forty years since Maesteg won the unofficial Championship in magnificent style. The unbeaten record which went with the title is an achievement matched only by Swansea and Newport among the major Welsh clubs. In the days before television and instant radio reportage, news of the team's

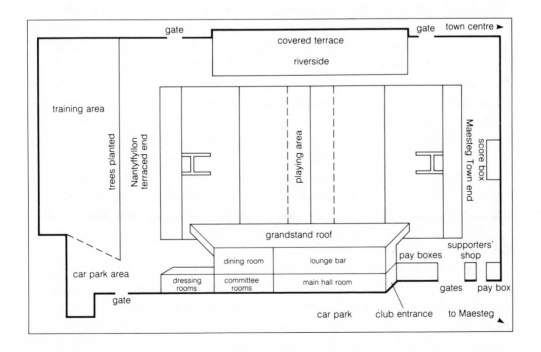

final result of the season, a 6–6 draw with Neath at the Gnoll, was flashed on the local cinema screen. The audience shunned the Hollywood spectacular due to be shown and flocked to join the huge throng gathering to greet the returning heroes at the railway station. The news raced around the Rugby world and even reached America, where Welsh exiles raised money for a golden commemorative ball to be presented to the men of the Old Parish.

Nothing quite so glamorous has since befallen Maesteg, though they were strong enough between 1977 and 1979 to take the Whitbread Merit Table title. But they have endured as a powerful strong-point of uncompromising Valleys Rugby, supplying Welsh Internationals, some British Lions – and the occasional shock result. In their Centenary year they held the powerful Maori tourists to a 10–10 draw.

Infrastructure was not a word used by planners in the nineteenth century. The Llynfi Valley's scattered farmsteads and cottages were augmented by a rapid growth of small homesteads for workers in the flourishing ironworks which began operations in 1826, but for decades a simple tramroad was the main method of transportation between the growing town of Maesteg – 'Fairfield' – and the harbours along the coast. And well into the twentieth century the drive up the valley was a long and tortuous one along roads which scarcely accommodated the growing volume of traffic. Hence for long, a fixture with the club presented an unusually chilling prospect: first an undeniably wearisome journey; afterwards the trip back again; with, in between, an eighty-minute ordeal at the hands of raw-boned forwards and hard-tackling backs. It used to be all too much for some fashionable but fastidious clubs and their star players.

That has all changed since the completion a decade ago of the M4 and its associated road systems. Now it is but a fifteen-minute run from the motorway to the little town and the Rugby club perched on a flattened tip above it. The Old Parish ground presents a reassuringly modern appearance to visitors with its neat grandstand (complete with recently-installed television deck), covered terrace, lush turf, floodlights dating back to 1964, and ample reception rooms. But the basic ingredients of Maesteg's welcome remain constant: the welcome is warm – and the Rugby tough.

The club has its museum, trophy room and rows of team photographs – and also a badge that can start tongues wagging. Its 'fiery castle' – recalling the storming of Castell Coch at Llangynwyd – was worn by the Glamorgan longbowmen at Agincourt. Also depicted are the figures 7777. The story goes that a local stonemason was commissioned to inscribe the headstone of a Maesteg woman who had died at the age of twenty-eight. Unable to produce satisfactory curves for the numerals, he reasoned that twenty-eight was made up of four sevens and settled for the series of straight incisions required for the Rugby club's emblem. It might be concluded that the deceased was the wife of a committeeman.

After moving from the town cricket ground to their present premises in 1900, the club could claim to be firmly established by 1914 when David Watts won four Welsh caps. The story of the 'twenties and 'thirties is a familiar one, with economic hardship and an accompanying downturn in spirits and morale hitting south Wales. Many people from the Valleys were forced to emigrate to earn a living, and Maesteg lost players to the League code.

This was a period when they owed their very survival to the unstinting efforts of one man, Enoch Rees, whose inspired management during the dark days ensured that the Old Parish would move straight into top gear with the arrival of better times in post-war Wales. Rees was a national selector for ten years, represented Wales on the International Board, and was honoured with life membership of the Welsh Rugby Union after his Presidency in 1957.

Maesteg's affable President, Windsor Major (whom along with Trevor Rees I have always classed as the welcoming duo) was capped by Wales in 1949 and again in 1950 as a member of the splendid Championship side whose full record comprised thirty-seven victories and six draws. The reward for skipper Trevor Lloyd was a cap at scrum half for Wales and a history-making trip to South Africa which he toured in 1955 as the first member of his club to become a British Lion. Cliff Howe, tearaway Leighton Davies, Ray 'Chico' Hopkins and Gwyn Evans were the outstanding men of the next couple of decades, while in 1977–78 smooth-running wing Colin Donovan made a hit with thirty-seven record-breaking tries in his first season. Since their Whitbread successes of that period Maesteg's accomplishments have been less eye-catching, but they remain capable of major efforts on big days and supplied prop Peter Francis to the Welsh front row for the Murrayfield match of 1987.

Their players have never been mere wearers of jerseys. In 1978 the then captain Billy Pole led a revolt against the decision not to award his men blazers and badges to mark their first Whitbread title. Fortunately the committee relented and the dispute was resolved in time for the season's fixtures to be completed.

Great Days at Llynfi Road

26.12.1976: Bridgend 11pts, Maesteg 21pts

Given that televised Rugby in Wales has normally comprised recorded highlights, the live excitement of a Schweppes Cup draw gave a boost to the Sunday afternoon programmes I once presented. But so often it was *déjà vu* as far as Bridgend and Maesteg were concerned. The little balls extracted from the velvet bag have bracketed the two old rivals together no fewer than six times at important junctures of the competition – and each time Bridgend have won. Sometimes the margin has been comfortable, once or twice nail-bitingly close as in 1985 when the result was 9–9 only for Bridgend to go through on the try they scored.

So it is pleasant to recall a match which saw the Old Parish's first win at the Brewery Field for eight years. Robert Stephens and Wayne Morris scored tries for the visitors, lanky Gwyn Evans placing thirteen points with goal kicks. Maesteg completed a double on Easter Saturday and went on to win the next four matches against their old, close rivals.

27.10.1982: Maesteg 10pts, Maoris 10pts

Having swept Cardiff aside in their opening fixture, the Maoris managed by Waka Nathan were favourites to win the Centenary fixture at Llynfi Road against their first Valleys opponents. In the event the Old Parish fought them all the way and emerged with a creditable draw.

The match was a personal triumph for the burly centre Phil Phillips, captaining his club in their hundredth season and ably abetted on this occasion by back row forward David Arthur's leadership of a gritty pack. Until late in the game the tourists led through tries by Baker and Woodman, the former adding a conversion, against penalties by Ian Hall. Spurred on by the 7000 crowd, however, Maesteg mounted a final onslaught which was crowned with success when Phillips battered his way through a series of tackles for a great equalising score.

Maesteg's Heroes

The first of Maesteg's Welsh caps went to miner **David Watts**, a lock forward who played against England, Scotland, Ireland and France in 1914 as a member of the 'Terrible Eight'. Watts lost his life in World War I, but **Aaron Rees** and **Evan Davies** survived to be picked against the 1919 New Zealand Army XV.

Trevor Lloyd reversed the journey taken by so many Welsh stars, moving from the Taibach suburb of Aberavon to further his career at Maesteg. The move paid off.

Lloyd was a hard-working and technically accomplished scrum half, good at coaxing and cajoling forwards from close range. He nursed his men through the long, demanding campaign of 1949–50 and won caps in 1953 in the absence of Rex Willis. Two years later Lloyd was a surprise selection for the British Isles tour party to South Africa, and followed this up by captaining his country in the seventy-fifth anniversary match between Wales and the Lions in 1955.

Raymond 'Chico' Hopkins flitted across the Welsh scene like an amiable comet. His honorary membership of the 'Arlequins RFC is thought to be the first such honour conferred upon anyone from the Llynfi Valley, and in the two or three seasons before turning professional he charmed the Rugby world with his mixture of dry wit, good clean fun, and his robust approach to working the scrums.

Had he not been a contemporary of Gareth Edwards he would have added to the single cap he won as a replacement at Twickenham in 1970. On that occasion Edwards's retirement with a leg injury gave 'Chico' a chance he boldly seized, scoring a try and helping to swing the game away from England's grip for a 17–13 win. The Lions took him to New Zealand in 1971 where he was once more a replacement for Edwards, this time in the all-important First Test which the tourists won 9–3.

Hopkins joined Swinton Rugby League club in 1972.

Gwyn Evans was a most elegant player who could turn in an expert performance virtually anywhere in the back division. After a serious knee operation which checked his early progress, he moved steadily up the Welsh ladder via Schools and B caps to play ten full Internationals for Wales between 1981 and 1983, travelling to New Zealand in the latter years as utility back.

Evans was the most reliable of goal-kickers, equalling the world record for Test matches with six penalties against France at Cardiff in 1982.

PENARTH RFC

HQ: Penarth Athletic Ground
Strip: Blue

The Bears with the sore head: I agonised long and hard over the decision to accord Penarth the full treatment in this volume.

The blunt truth is that for many seasons the club have failed to deliver the goods. Members of the Whitbread Merit Table as a result of their original

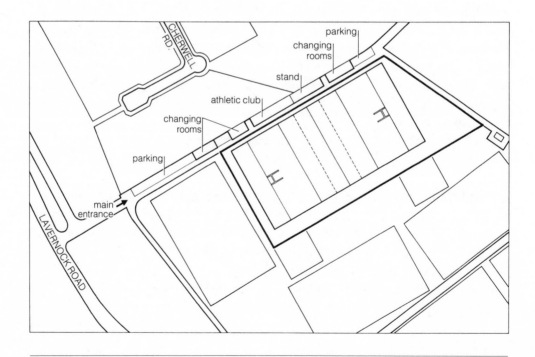

association with the Snelling Sevens group, they have yet to win more than three Merit Table matches in any one season. Their Schweppes Cup record has been abysmal (in 1988 it was Gwent village Blackwood who proved too high a first hurdle). No International player has emerged from their ranks since the 'thirties and Jack Bassett's heyday. They have lost their traditional Easter Friday fixture with the Barbarians. They frequently go down to defeat by fifty, sixty or even eighty points. And their President, Irishman George Moore, is on record as saying, 'We are a club going nowhere with nowhere to go.'

Many would agree with that last sentiment, and argue that they should be put out to the grass of junior and district Rugby. Cynics suggest that they retain their Merit Table status only because fellow clubs enjoy the chance of running in seven or eight tries and building up their bid for the monthly cash bonuses which reward heavy scoring. Discernibly Penarth players these days take the field expecting defeat; they recognise that they are the chopping block.

Do they, then, deserve the 'first-class' status which, in the media at least, they still enjoy? Why distinguish them from the multitude of grass-roots clubs who frolic happily in the substrata of Welsh Rugby? Is there anything more to the Seasiders than an afterglow of great days?

Just as it is right to dwell on the rise of some clubs, who began in small ways but have forced their way to the front rank, so it appears reasonable to me on reflection to give space to one which still retains trappings of style and success but whose star is in decline. Sympathy, sentiment and the brotherhood of the Rugby game comes into it; plus awareness that tides can turn.

Somehow, Penarth need to acquire the new dynamic which has been missing for two decades. Such direction seems unlikely to come from the present committee, which is almost as large as the playing strength and has perpetrated collective errors of judgement. It would be unfair to expect initiatives from the accomplished chairman of recent years, Kevin Bush, who took control as a stop-gap in 1975 and has loyally stayed on adding to the seasons of tremendous service that he gave as a player – one good enough to be chosen for a Final Welsh Trial. As for the players, because tails are down, current team members can be forgiven for feeling that the priority is to survive rather than to rock the boat with demands for radical reform.

Nor, despite the generosity which is often manifested in terms of sponsorship, can the club turn with confidence to the 40,000 local inhabitants for an injection of confidence. Though ostensibly a self-contained town, separated from Cardiff by the River Ely, Penarth is curiously suburban. To outsiders it does not seem bothered about inspiring effort and achievement in the interests of its good name. It must be the only place of its size in the United Kingdom that does not boast an Association Football club playing competitive or league football, in contrast to Barry and little Sully just down the coast. There is an absence of that innate fervour which characterises Valley communities of the same size, sustaining creativity and morale through thick and thin.

Someone told me, 'This club needs a Messiah.' Perhaps, in the first place, a Pied Piper might be a better proposition – to lead the youngsters of Penarth in the direction of the Athletic Ground. The town has two giant-sized secondary schools, St Cyres and Stanwell, which regularly produce well-tutored teams and fine players. But in the last decade men like Owen Golding, Steve Crandon, Mike Goldsworthy, Peter Goodfellow and Ian Eidman have gone elsewhere to win their spurs and not a few Welsh caps. Penarth need to find a way of attracting such talent. That should not be beyond the bounds of possibility – school team-mates often enjoy playing senior Rugby in each other's company (hence the success of the Old Penarthians just across the road from the Athletic Ground); but it requires that an initiative be taken.

There is, too, the Vale of Glamorgan's vast hinterland. Here are more schools turning out Rugby products of good quality. Here live raw-boned farmers with energy to burn and muscle-power to fuel the blaze. Here are folk imbued with a desire to play the best Rugby available and to compete against top opposition. Such a repository should be scoured by a club that takes itself and its future seriously.

The arrival of leagues in Welsh Rugby could be the re-making or breaking of Penarth. Thanks to their membership of the Whitbread group they will start in a favoured Second Division position. Then it will be up to them: to consolidate and achieve a genuine status based on results and be perceived again by potential recruits as a going concern; or to slide slowly out of contention as a force to be reckoned with.

The ball is in their half. There is a fund of goodwill upon which new coach Billy Griffiths, skipper Mark Owen and stalwarts Baden Evans, Bob Dyer and Gareth John can draw. But it will not last forever.

Penarth RFC have an act to get together.

Great Days at the Athletic Ground

3.4.1976: Penarth 36pts, Barbarians 30pts

Of all the richly entertaining fixtures between Penarth and their traditional Good Friday opponents, this was surely the greatest from the home side's point of view. Lyn Baxter's side were lined up as a first course for the tourists' Easter feast of Rugby, to be gobbled up greedily; instead, with scrum half Dennis John in tremendous form, Penarth recorded a third post-war victory over the Baa-Baas, running up a highest-ever score.

Dennis John (2), Mike Chinnock (2), Selwyn Phillips, Joe Davies and Alan Stamp got the home side's tries, with John converting four.

28.3.1986: Penarth 15pts, Barbarians 39pts

The Barbarians fired a thirty-nine gun salute to Penarth as they signed off after a series of matches which began in 1901. Pressure upon players from overseas tour demands was the prime excuse for the ending of a fond relationship.

The tourists scored eight tries, three of them by sprightly Lansdowne hooker Willie Burns. Nick Wall and Huw Rees registered the final tries for Penarth. In the 85-year span the home side won eleven matches against fifty-nine by their opponents. There were four drawn games.

Heroes of Penarth

The outstanding figure in Penarth's 110-year history was **Jack Bassett**, a full back who led Wales nine times between 1929 and 1932, when he won the last of his fifteen caps. Bassett also travelled with the 1930 British Lions to Australia and New Zealand, where he made four Test appearances.

This sturdy policeman is remembered for devastating tackling. But in later years he turned to watching Association Football, and was always reticent about discussing his great Rugby feats. He died early in 1989.

Though not an International, **Bernard** ('Slogger') **Templeman** was undoubtedly one of Rugby football's larger-than-life characters in his heyday. An orthodox scrum half in his early days with Penarth, he later developed an amazing skill at dropping goals from that most difficult of positions – he once put over three against Newport at Rodney Parade.

He skippered the club in 1960 and led them to a 10–8 victory over the Barbarians, the first for forty years. These days he is often to be seen in the Market area of central Cardiff – where, if he commands your presence at a congenial tavern, you go meekly.

PONTYPRIDD RFC

HQ: Sardis Road
Strip: Black and white hoops

You know you are in Rugby territory the moment you leave the A470 and head into Pontypridd. The entrance to a double-fronted building, where strong ale looks as if it might be on sale, is guarded by giant casts of J.P.R. Williams and Gerald Davies. The windows are festooned with replicas of players from the four corners of the

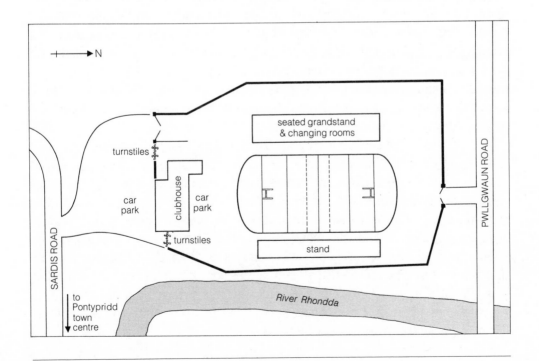

earth: Mourie, Porta, McBride, Beaumont, Irvine, Campese, Blanco are all there, not to mention Gareth Edwards, Tom David and the Pontypool front row. Inside, china clay midgets stand in grim-staring ranks.

This is John Hughes's unique 'grogg' shop. Many nations have their Rugby cartoonists (though few as gifted as the *South Wales Echo*'s Gren); but none boasts a potter-caricaturist like this son of a miner who took up his unique craft after becoming tired of local government. His products are treasured by the players themselves, they sell to Rugby folk all over the world, and some fanatics have even asked to be buried with a 'Gareth' or 'Barry' beside them in the coffin.

It takes a good deal to tear yourself away from the Hughes establishment. Fortunately the Rugby entertainment on offer a mile away at Sardis Road provides enough incentive.

The bont (bridge) emblems perched on Pontypridd's posts, celebrating the architectural merit of the old structure which was once the main crossing of the Taff hereabouts, make a colourful decorative detail. Today they are not, perhaps, quite so jaunty as in the days a decade ago when the club were winning Championship titles and reaching Cup Finals. Yet at Sardis Road an immense amount of quiet consolidation has taken place following those euphoric days. The grandstand has been extended and infrastructured with comfortable changing quarters and lounges. More space has been provided over at the clubhouse, with a streamlining of bars and social facilities. And supporters have responded with loyalty and enthusiasm: an evening fixture in midweek with top opponents like Cardiff or a cup-tie against Llanelli can draw 7000 spectators to watch the action, sometimes under brilliant floodlights. Pontypridd has acquired the swagger of a major Rugby centre.

But not without sweat and hard graft. Nine of their first ten decades' existence were spent climbing the ladder of respectability from humble beginnings at Taff Vale Park and People's Park, via Ynysangharad Park (sacrificed in 1971 for a dual carriageway development) to the snug hillside arena which is Sardis Road. The awarding of caps to Pontypridd players were isolated occurrences, and the fixture list grew but slowly. The watershed came in the 1959–60 season which yielded twenty nine splendid victories and was a springboard for the Championship title that followed in 1962–63. Since then a succession of strong administrators like Sam Simon, Graham Gittins and quiet-spoken secretary Stan Thomas, have watched over a period of consolidation which has brought Whitbread Merit Table distinction and near misses in a Schweppes Cup Final.

Above: Phil Bennett, a brilliant runner from broken play. The three giant All Blacks will find him hard to corner

Right: Mervyn Davies: his trademarks on the field were a bristling bandit moustache and a broad swathe of white bandage

Above: Barbarians versus New Zealand, 1973. Gareth Edwards, scorer of the glorious opening try, senses the emerging opportunity from over Derek Quinnell's shoulder. John Dawes has drawn Sid Going (9) and is releasing to Tom David, with John Pullin close at hand

Below: Fiji at Stradey Park, full of flair and fallibility. Llanelli's victory over the tourists in 1985 eclipsed all others for sheer improbability

Right: Scottish defenders close in on Wales's Ray Gravell, a centre whose play was characterised by passion and commitment

Below: Wales v. Scotland, 1982: a magnificent study of Bob Norster showing, on his first appearance for Wales, the form which has enabled him to dominate line out jumping in the nineteen eighties

Graham Price is remembered as an outstanding scrummager. But here he is about to take line out ball from the French

In the nineteen eighties Cardiff emerged as a force in the Schweppes Cup. Here John Scott is triumphant after the 1981 victory over Bridgend

A fine study of the multi-talented Mark Ring

An occasional chip can still be discerned on the club's broad shoulders, mainly exposed by the perceived myopia of the Welsh selectors. Exciting Jonathan Mason, a full back worth 312 points to his side in 1987–88, became their latest cap when he travelled to New Zealand in the summer and played in the Second Test – but why, Pontypridd wanted to know, was he not in the original tour selection, which included two men who had played just fourteen games in the position between them? In autumn 1988 the omission of hooker Phil John from the Wales B XV against France also rankled: 'Unfortunately we are well used in Pontypridd to this treatment from the national selectors,' wrote the editor of their match programme. 'Let us hope that this is only a momentary lapse on their part not to pick the players in form.'

Pontypridd's bad luck has been to lie on the road leading from the Rhondda Valleys down to Cardiff, and many key players have either by-passed the club altogether on their way to the glamour of Rugby on the coast or, like Dannie Harris, learned their trade before moving on elsewhere. Even Tom David had to go west and join Llanelli to gain International recognition, though his subsequent return to Sardis Road for his final fling in the Union game provided the impetus for memorable Championship triumphs in 1978 and 1979.

But at Pontypridd there have always been glorious exceptions, and there probably always will be. Their need in the 'nineties will be for a play-maker in the David mould who will attract youngsters to play with and around him – and remain in the fold.

Great Days at Pontypridd

24.2.1979: Pontypridd 9pts, Cardiff 7pts

Pontypridd took the unofficial Championship title by just 0.62% in 1978–79. But runners-up Bridgend beat them fairly and squarely in the Schweppes Cup Final, when by their own admission big-match nerves overcame many players. So at Sardis Road they prefer to remember the Fourth Round defeat of neighbouring giants Cardiff, whose 18–0 victory the previous Boxing Day was avenged.

Cardiff played a tight forward game backed by the strong breaks of Terry Holmes at scrum half who grabbed an unconverted try. A slick move between half backs Robin Morgan and Stuart Lewis set up Pontypridd's winning try, converted by Colin Bolderson. They knocked out Aberavon 6–3 in a thrilling semi-final.

This was a season when Ian Walsh showed flair at full back, the experience of

John Poole and Jeff Hazzard was always useful in midfield, and Tom David led a robust pack in which Chris Seldon and the brothers Shellard, Mike and David, were always to the fore.

26.9.1979: Pontypridd 3pts, Romania 9pts

The dour Romanians, who were soon to thrash Wales in Bucharest, caught the champion club cold in September and grafted their way to a notable win. Torrential rain hampered Pontypridd's attempts to run the ball, their best attacks being cut down by opponents who proved expert at launching swift counters.

Despite the weather, 5500 loyal supporters turned out to watch, and had grounds for optimism at half time when the scores were level at a penalty goal apiece. The tourists finished the stronger, however, a Bucos penalty plus Dumitru's dropped goal seeing them through.

Pontypridd's Heroes

Five Pontypridd men were capped by Wales between 1881 and the start of World War I. Thirty-five long years then passed before **Glyn Davies** burst upon the scene. Partnered by fellow sixth former Wynford Davies against England in the Victory International match of 1946, this dashing stand off half won the first of his eleven full caps the following year in Wales's 22–8 win at Murrayfield.

Davies was an attacking player with sure hands and a devastating side-step off both feet. After his grooming at Pontypridd he appeared with distinction for Cambridge University, the Army and the Barbarians. His career with a leading wine company took him to Bristol, where he put in several seasons at the Memorial Ground before ending his playing days with Glamorgan Wanderers. He died suddenly, and prematurely, in 1976.

The Welsh selectors of his day vacillated between Davies's attacking genius and the pin-point accuracy of W.B. Cleaver's tactical kicking, with the result that the elegant Pontypridd man's international place was never sure. Time finally ran out for him in 1951 when he took the rap for his country's unexpectedly heavy defeat in Edinburgh.

Russell Robins was the exception to the rule that all Pontypridd players have to move before winning regular recognition from the selectors. Until joining Leeds

Rugby League club in 1958 he remained a one-club man, holding the captaincy for three seasons.

In addition to strapping physique, Robins's attributes included sure handling skills which made him thus equally at home at lock or number eight forward. It was in the latter position that he impressed South African critics on the Lions' tour of 1955 with its drawn Test series. He won thirteen Welsh caps.

The Llanelli band-wagon gained an unexpected recruit when **Tom David** joined it in 1971. The club certainly benefited from the back row booster effect of the David presence; and the move paid off, too, for the player, who was able to fine-tune his game under the influence of Carwyn James and the Scarlets' think-tank. He made successful Cup Final appearances, became a Barbarian (playing in the memorable 1973 defeat of New Zealand), was elected Player of the Year, won four caps and toured with the British Isles in South Africa.

But David, a barrel-chested brigand of a forward, with a lazy eye and a lazy voice to go with it, is forever associated with Pontypridd. As a youngster he was an 80-minute player for his side and later, after the seasons at Stradey Park, returned to lead and inspire it to the thrilling title triumphs of 1978 and 1979. Perhaps his only big disappointment came in the 1979 Schweppes Final when Pontypridd fell to Bridgend – who included his business partner and good pal Steve Fenwick.

Rangy lock forward **Bob Penberthy** epitomised economy in motion. While never appearing to exert himself unduly, he regularly took line out ball from the toughest opponents in the land. The secret lay in the precise way in which he positioned himself to jump, allied to a keen sense of timing.

A great servant of his club, Penberthy played his first senior game while still captain of Pontypridd Youth in 1961. By his retirement in 1986 he had totalled an astonishing 876 matches, holding the captaincy for three seasons, and winning a Barbarian jersey late in his career.

THE
GWENT
CONNECTION

ABERTILLERY RFC

HQ: Abertillery Park
Strip: Green and white hoops

The Rugby men of Gwent were hopping mad in April 1988. Wales's New Zealand tour party contained just four men from the county's clubs: Mark Ring, Kevin Moseley and Staff Jones from Pontypool along with Ebbw Vale's hooker Ian Watkins. A host of people, by no means confined to south-east Wales, considered

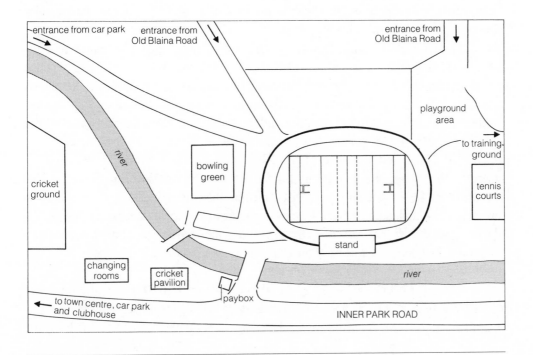

it an inexplicably low tally. The situation acquired a grotesque aspect when, in the final analysis taking in the choice of replacements, it was noted that the representation from the whole of Gwent was matched by that of South Wales Police, whom nobody with the best will in the world could deem better than good Mid Glamorgan triers. Such a blow, both to pride and to confidence in the way players' skill and ability are assessed by national selectors, is bound to take a long time to mend.

This point having been made, however, it should be stated that the hot-bed of the game which comprises the eastern and western valleys of Gwent contains a disproportionately large number of would-be centres of excellence; and there are some who say that this leads to a dissipation of the available talent. In the south are Cross Keys, Cwmbran, Rogerstone and Croesyceiliog. Pontypool, Newbridge, Risca, Crumlin, Pontnewydd, Abercarn, Garndiffaith, Talywain, Llanhilleth, Blackwood, Bargoed and Pontypool United cluster further up-country. Ebbw Vale, Rhymney, Cwmtillery, Blaina, Blaenavon and the steelmen of RTB are to be found along the so-called Heads of the Valleys where the snow-line lies just behind the goalposts.

In itself such a plethora of clubs is tremendously healthy and means that newcomers are always knocking at the doors of the senior clubs in the county. Out of those noted, no fewer than four claim first-class status and also possess the fixture lists to underwrite it. That is an estimable state of affairs and speaks volumes for the giant strides those clubs took two or three decades ago. Nowadays, however, with fewer young men coming into the game and an ever-increasing number of counter-attractions, there may not quite be the genuine talent to support such a complement of top-ranked clubs (and we have not mentioned Newport, down between the estuaries of Usk and Ebbw). It will be interesting to see whether Gwent's leading clubs can take into the twenty-first century the fixtures they first secured back in the nineteen fifties or earlier.

The list above left out Abertillery RFC, a club which would be the first to concede the point. Life is hard in this hill village in northern Gwent. The Government in its wisdom, recently warned that Abertillery might become a 'disaster town' unless positive steps were taken to halt local economic decline. No player from the Rugby club has represented Wales since the 'sixties. Gates are measured in hundreds rather than thousands. No major title has been won for nearly sixty years.

Yet Abertillery have a lot going for them, not least the former station hotel which was turned into a clubhouse three decades ago and which was recently bought outright. Here can be seen the obligatory display cabinets and honours boards, repositories of club pride and tradition. Here are faded sepia photographs recalling the heyday of Bedwellty Jones, a member of the pre-World War I 'terrible eight', Hocker Thomas and their iron-hard contemporaries. Here are more recent portraits in colour featuring the great back row forwards Alun Pask and Haydn Morgan.

Then there is Abertillery Park, a few hundred yards from the clubhouse, which must be among the two or three most dramatic Rugby grounds in the United Kingdom. Steep terracing, above which the mountainside rises sheerly, lends it the aspect of an amphitheatre. And just occasionally, as when Japan visited Abertillery during their 1983 Centenary season, there is a crowd worthy of it. Bigger midweek attendances can be anticipated with the installation of new floodlighting first used in autumn 1988.

But a key resource is the energy Abertillery have managed to generate in the 'eighties which projected them from bottom of the pile to fifth and sixth positions in the Championship tables for 1987 and 1988. They prepared a well-publicised five-year plan, which involved launching a mini-Rugby scheme, a Colts XV and re-forming the Athletic XV. The aim is to maintain the new momentum with a flow of home-produced youngsters brimful of club pride.

Modern Rugby at Abertillery is uneven in quality. But the club possesses undeniable resilience stemming from personality – and from its characters: men like gallant Malcolm Lewis, three times the victim of a broken leg, giant Ian Brice (who must have been capped had he been more mean), Mike Cairns, Ray Gladwyn, Brian Wilkins and Martin Brickell.

Abertillery is not normally considered cosmopolitan. However, Scottish International E.C. Fahmy played for them in the 'twenties. And once, presumably en route from Belfast to Bloemfontein, it is recorded that W.J. McBride turned out against Newbridge.

Great Days at Abertillery Park

25.12.1908: Abertillery 3pts, Australia 3pts

The First Wallabies of 1908–09 compared unfavourably with the All Blacks and Springboks who had just made inaugural tours. Nonetheless Dr A.M. Moran's team recorded wins over such important opponents as England, Cornwall, Gloucestershire, Durham and Glamorgan, but were held to a 3–3 draw at Abertillery Park.

Man of the match for the home side was Billy Bowen who scored the all-important try. A lapel badge was struck to commemorate a marvellous Christmas Day achievement.

8.10.1983: Abertillery 13pts, Japan 17pts

Fixtures against major touring sides are precious and for many a long decade Abertillery found themselves linked with other Gwent sides such as Ebbw Vale when the All Blacks or Springboks were in the land – and were usually brushed aside by the tourists. The Springboks of 1931 and 1960, however, who won 10–9 and 3–0, did not regard such teams as pushovers.

The game against Japan was thus awarded to Abertillery in recognition of the club's Centenary. The Japs had been wiped off the face of the earth on their previous tour, and five thousand spectators came expecting to see Abertillery eat them for lunch. By 1983, however, the wearers of the cherry blossom were made of sterner – and bigger – stuff and they ran in two superb tries and kicked their goals to lead at one stage by 17–0.

Then, as Kevin Clark placed a trio of neat penalty goals, a perfect chip to the corner by Dave George engineered a try for wing David Owen. Though they finished just the stronger, Abertillery failed to gain an equalising try.

Abertillery's Heroes

His twenty-seven caps make **Wick** (short for **Wickham**) **Powell** the second most capped Welsh scrum half of all time after Gareth Edwards. His name is more readily associated with London Welsh, Wasps and the Army, but he was born at Aberbeeg and turned out a number of times for the club just three miles up the Valley. Powell was a big, powerful man with a tremendous length of pass.

The russet-haired **Haydn Morgan** burst upon the scene in 1958 when he won the first of his twenty-seven caps. He was a destroyer-flanker in the old tradition, staying out of forward confrontations in order to make life a misery for opposing midfield players. Much was made of the fact that as a National Serviceman he had served as a paratrooper – and certainly stand off halves who went for a gap that appeared were often clobbered from out of the blue.

The Morgan International career spanned eight years during which he collected twenty-seven caps and went on two Lions tours. Few opponents gave him the run-around, an exception being the brilliant Richard Sharp whose breaks past a stale-looking Morgan set up a memorable and unexpected win for England over Wales at Twickenham in 1960.

Allan Lewis enjoyed a volatile but short-lived career at scrum half for Wales. He came into the team sensationally, displacing the 1965 Triple Crown captain Clive Rowlands and going on the Lions tour of 1966. Equally abruptly he was in turn replaced in 1967 by the young Gareth Edwards.

He continued to serve his club for many subsequent seasons so that the youngsters of Abertillery had ample opportunity to study his model passing off sturdy, well-planted legs.

Allan's brother **Malcolm Lewis** might have won caps had he not suffered three leg fractures at crucial moments in his career. As it was, he was for long a member of the finest club back row in the land along with Haydn Morgan and **Alun Pask**.

Like Morgan a paratrooper, the last-named was a tall, mobile number eight forward with enough bulk to anchor a scrummage securely. He was effective at the line out, but the memorable feature of his play was his speed about the open field in support of his backs. Pask's handling was also of the highest order.

He was a regular scorer in club games, and picked up two tries for Wales including a bravura effort at Twickenham in 1966. That winter, as captain of Wales, he was favourite to lead the British Isles in New Zealand, but an unexpected failure by Wales in Dublin probably wrecked his chances, Mike Campbell-Lamerton gaining the selectors' vote.

Pask is the last player to have been capped from Abertillery, though Robert Norster founded his career with the club before moving to Cardiff.

CROSS KEYS RFC

HQ: Pandy Park
Strip: Black and white hoops

Whatever slings and arrows they endure, whatever life's stress and pressures, however much time they spend lodged near the foot of the unofficial Championship table, Cross Keys can always look back proudly on The Day They Defeated Wales.

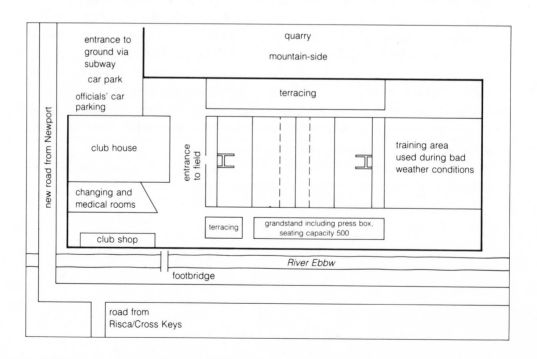

December 1926 found the club in dire straits, with the Western Valley desperately hard up after the summer's coal strike. The Welsh Rugby Union declined to meet Cross Keys' anguished appeal for a cash loan to stay in business, but agreed to send an International XV to play a special fund-raising match which took place the following March. Pandy Park was packed, the future of the club was assured – and Cross Keys won by thirteen points to eight.

In those days there were giants in the land. Cross Keys were usually represented in the International fifteens of the period and the power of their forward play was unsurpassed. They took the Championship title in 1922 and 1926 and again in 1936.

But the Depression had arrived. A whole generation moved away from south-east Wales and especially the old industrial areas. New blood was thus thin; and, where it manifested itself, it often ebbed away to the Rugby League code which offered a good living, albeit far away. This brawn-drain caused Cross Keys grievous, though thanks to the hard work and dedication of its members not mortal, suffering. But the club's achievements between the wars represent its zenith; and they have never since been matched.

The Pandy Park of today, while hardly a Superbowl, is one of the cosiest and compact club grounds to be found anywhere in the world. It lies ensconced below a high, gaunt quarry close to the confluence of the rivers Ebbw and Sirhowy, and Cross Keys have used it since the turn of the century. In those early days it was a focal point for the miners of Nine Mile Point, Risca and Cwmcarn collieries to take weekend exercise and fill their lungs with fresh air. The character of the Western Valley has changed radically down the years, with light industry the main sources of employment today, but the village Rugby club is still a social centre of importance.

It is also easy for outsiders to reach, lying close to the new dual carriageway linking Newport with the Heads of the Valleys. And the roadworks of the early nineteen eighties did the Rugby club an indirect favour. A strip of Pandy Park was commandeered by the engineers, compensation was paid out, and the cash helped to fund the imposing new clubhouse and changing rooms built for £300,000 and opened in 1981 – when Trevor Williams, a Cross Keys member of the Wales XV that beat New Zealand in 1935, was served with the first pint. Another sign of prosperity is the magnificent bank of floodlights. The grandstand backing onto the Ebbw is small but comfortable while the hillside opposite forms a natural terrace. The day of the 5000 gate is over for the foreseeable future (with rare exceptions), but an attractive fixture still pulls in enough spectators to complete the sense of theatre.

Cross Keys' most pressing need today is to recapture the consistency of old. They have spent the 1980s in the bottom five of the unofficial Championship. They are regularly swept out of the Schweppes Cup's early rounds. They really could do with a run of success in the Cup or Championship competitions which would raise morale and capture young players' imagination.

For in recent years many of the more talented ones have clearly looked on Pandy Park as a staging post or launch pad. The Cross Keys archives contain many names which acquired more lustre as part of other clubs' team-sheets: Stuart Watkins, Gareth Evans, Bobby Windsor and Tony Faulkner are just some.

Great Days at Pandy Park

30.3.1927: Cross Keys 13pts, Wales XV 8pts

Les Perkins and the Cross Keys forwards were the vital factors which swung this historic match in the club's favour. The former, a strong running centre, got one of his side's three tries, to which the International XV could reply only with a goal and a penalty goal.

9.10.1985: Cross Keys 12pts, Fiji 26pts

Down the years Cross Keys have usually met touring sides in harness with Abertillery or Pontypool. With the exception of the 1931 game against the Third Springboks, lost by just a point, the arrangement failed consistently to provide a satisfactory contest.

Cross Keys also lost their first solo match against front-rank tourists, going down 12–26 in the first match of the 1985 Fijians' tour. But the occasion, televised live, was memorable, not least to the tourists who spoke in glowing terms both of the welcome they received and also the standard of Cross Keys' resistance. Well they might, for their front five were pressurised into disastrous retreats and collapses by the aggressive front row work of Phil Leader and Richie Donovan – who were still going strongly enough at the close to claim a penalty try as the tourists dropped a scrummage.

Before that, however, Fiji had scored three sparkling tries which delighted a big crowd filling the stand and terracing – and overflowing onto the hillside above.

Cross Keys' Heroes

Because of the constant movement of key players to nearby clubs in a higher echelon, it is a long time since Cross Keys could point to a truly outstanding figure in their ranks over a long period of time. Glyn Bram, Brian Anthony, Kerry Williams and Derek Church have rendered valiant service in the recent past, and the tireless flanker Nick Parkes made his mark with a record fourteen tries in 1987–88. But most of the club's heroes are old-timers.

Steve Morris was the first man from Cross Keys to win a Welsh cap, appearing nineteen times between 1920 and 1925 as a lock or flanker. He captained the National XV, and when his International career ended abruptly there was speculation at Pandy Park that his robust approach had caused him to fall foul of the authorities of the other Home Unions who had asked for his dismissal. Be that as it may, he was chosen for the England-Wales Invitation XV which played Scotland-Ireland on The Close in 1924 to celebrate a hundred years of the handling game at Rugby School.

Ron Herrera, born within a few yards of Pandy Park, was the second of a great triumvirate who represented Cross Keys in the 'twenties and 'thirties. A versatile forward from Wattsville, he appeared at lock, prop and hooker in the course of winning eight caps between 1925 and 1927.

Herrera is remembered for one feat in particular: on February 6, 1926 he scored the first try by a Welshman at Scotland's new Murrayfield headquarters. Wales lost, however, by eight points to five.

Then there was **Fred Bowdler** (known in the Western Valley as 'Lonza') who joined Cross Keys from Abercarn, where he worked as a miner, in 1926–27. He made his International debut against the Waratahs and went on to win fifteen caps at hooker. The Cross Keys club historian Horace Jefferies says Bowdler is remembered for his enormous appetite for match play. In days before floodlights he might turn out seventy times a season.

Among Cross Keys' most colourful characters was the tight forward **Rex Richards** who won a single cap against France in 1956. A crack swimmer (hence his nickname 'Tarzan') he left Wales to join a performing troupe in Florida, from where he returned occasionally to tour valley clubs and entertain with a guitar and a mellifluous singing voice.

EBBW VALE RFC

HQ: Eugene Cross Park
Strip: Red, green and white hoops

There is no doubt that Ebbw Vale will come up smelling of roses.

The 'eighties have been hard years for the Gwent steel town. The great plant at the head of the Ebbw Valley which not so long ago employed upwards of 12,000 men has been a pale imitation of its former self since the major recession which

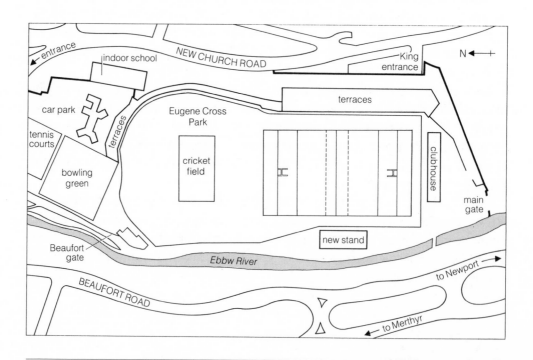

slashed world demand for the metal it forged. Tinplate is still made in the floor of the valley, and new production 'units' are establishing themselves on the windy foothills of the Brecon Beacons to the north. But the acres where Richard Thomas and Baldwin's great furnaces once roared and fiery coils sped their red-hot path along the rollers are now desolate. The gaunt hangars which sheltered them from the worst of the weather fell to the demolishers, earth-movers brushed away the debris, and now the terrain waits to be green again – planted with trees, shrubs, and hardy perennials which will be sturdy, mature growths by the time Ebbw Vale plays host to Britain's 1992 Garden Festival.

Such cataclysmic changes are inevitably affecting Ebbw Vale RFC whose health and fortunes have tended to contract along with local steel production. Absence of manpower has been the main problem with, first, a general outflow of population southwards and eastwards in search of work. Secondly, the powers-that-be at the Rugby club have no longer been able to lure promising recruits with safe jobs at the steelworks offering plenty of spare time to train and play to the greater glory of Ebbw Vale and Gwent. Thirdly the changing social pattern, admit Ebbw Vale officials sadly, has meant that many young men no longer wish to travel long distances on Saturdays even to top venues like Richmond, Coventry and Nottingham, preferring to attend the local Saturday night hop.

As if all this were not enough the passing of the Safety of Sports Grounds Act led to the condemnation of the club's elderly grandstand as unsafe and made necessary a long, expensive task of rebuilding (which was triumphantly executed). The clubhouse, too, was badly damaged by fire, its re-opening being delayed well into the autumn of 1988.

But hope springs eternal and these days Ebbw Vale can still reach a respectable mid-table place by season's end. With a loyal core of supporters, a determined committee, and a general air of returning prosperity along the Heads of the Valleys their future has potential.

The club's chequered history, however, will take some emulating. For example, after a few dismal years in the old Monmouthshire League around the turn of the century, Ebbw Vale turned to professional 13-a-side Rugby in an attempt to revive supporters' flagging interest. Before long the cost of fulfilling north country fixtures became prohibitive and for over a decade no Rugby football at all was played in the area. After World War I local interests approached the Welsh Rugby Union for a re-instatement of Ebbw Vale as an amateur club and, remarkably, their application was granted.

The valley groaned under Depression and all-pervading unemployment until RTB built their giant strip mill in the late 'thirties bringing new confidence and prosperity. Like coal, steel was an industry which had priority during World War II and Ebbw Vale used the available manpower to build a strong fixture list. This in turn enabled them to achieve first-class status in 1946, admission into the unofficial Welsh Championship following in 1949.

In the decade that ensued they could claim to be the dominant club, taking the title in 1952, 1954, 1957 and 1960. Men like Eugene Cross, after whom the 'Welfare Ground' was renamed in the 1970s, and Wally Talbot provided the administrative back-up, while on the field Ernie Lewis (later a first-class referee), Scotsman Arthur Smith and Graham Powell, the first Ebbw Vale man to win a cap, capitalised upon the work of robust forwards. By 1955, big bald Ben Edwards came back from Newport to kick the goals, a giant of a man with legs like tree trunks; so that all in all Ebbw Vale were a very complete Rugby machine.

For the kind of reasons mentioned at the outset, honours have escaped them since that time. The Valley's trauma sapped their natural resilience and will to succeed; inconsistency became the name of their game. But they have assets, notably a centrally-located ground, which witnessed the defeat of South Africa by Gwent back in 1969. Its ample terraces may yet overflow once more with supporters and enthusiasm if the Garden Festival and other Valleys initiatives yield the hoped-for harvest.

Great Days at Ebbw Vale

29.11.1960: Ebbw Vale/Abertillery 0pts, South Africa 3pts

Though Ebbw Vale were certainly worth a solo match against the Fifth Springboks their relatively late arrival on the first-class scene meant that they had to join forces with Abertillery, an unsatisfactory arrangement. Nevertheless in front of a packed house the combined XV put up a tremendous struggle against the tourists who were to lose only one match in the United Kingdom.

David Nash, the Vale's newest star, had been picked in the Wales XV to meet the Springboks the following Saturday and missed the game. His team-mates, however, gave a good account of themselves, notably stand off half Wilf Hunt whose diagonal kicking was a sound tactic on greasy turf. South Africa finally came through with a single try scored by wing Hennie van Zyl.

22.9.1979: Ebbw Vale 0pts, Romania 12pts

The allocation of this fixture against the first-ever Romanian side to visit Wales acknowledged Ebbw Vale's Centenary. Alas, the Rugby served up did not quite match the occasion. An edgy home team never mastered the dour, methodical tourists whose winning score comprised three penalties and a dropped goal.

Ebbw Vale's Heroes

Denzil Williams was just about the last of a long line of tough Welsh forwards who earned their living as steelworkers. That is, he brought immense power to his job in the tight but was undemonstrative and unflappable; he played with the Rugby equivalent of a poker face.

For a few years the big fellow, whose career spanned the 'sixties, was his country's most-capped forward. Though he appeared at lock for his club, his thirty-six caps were won at prop. He broke his customary low profile for Wales on one notable occasion during a Triple Crown contest against Ireland: Wales won a penalty, goal-kicking phenomenon Keith Jarrett stepped forward to take the ball, and the Irish retreated to their posts. Denzil Williams called for a tapped penalty, however, and thundered twenty yards for an important score against surprised opponents.

Centre **Arthur Lewis** came to prominence relatively late in his career as a twenty-eight-year-old member of the Gwent XV which beat the Springboks in 1969. On that day his clean-cut outside breaks were impressive, one of them leading to the try by Roger Beese which enabled the County to pull beyond reach of the tourists' challenge.

Eleven Welsh caps and a Lions tour to New Zealand quickly followed, though his style of play shifted more than marginally: he perfected a scissors move, usually with his stand off half, which often resulted in tries scored from close range. Even when he was held up, a close link would have been forged with support forwards. The ploy became known as an 'Arthur'.

Ebbw Vale has been served by a crop of fine forwards in the last twenty years who have been so near and yet so far from International selection. Into this category fall men such as Gareth Howls, Phil Gardner and Neil Robinson, the latter a skipper of the club for four successive seasons. Had they played for more 'fashionable' clubs they might well have been capped.

But **Clive Burgess** did break into the Welsh team in 1977 with a tearaway performance against Ireland climaxed by a spectacular try. He played four Internationals that season, but had to wait four years before collecting his other five caps. Burgess was a 'dog', that term of respect reserved for forwards who are never far from the ball, always well placed to block opponents, and ever ready to drop into the mud and kill a loose ball.

Ebbw Vale personnel have always been prepared to take their talents long distances for parading in front of appreciative and generous audiences. In the 'sixties Denzil Williams commuted regularly between the Heads of the Valleys and Vichy in southern France where, with Newport's Brian Price, he introduced some steel into the performance of the town pack. Burgess, for his part, chose the northern Italian centre of Breschia for a couple of seasons in the evening of his career.

And **Ian Watkins** is the Vale's latest International, a man who specialises in dramatic entries. In his first Cup-tie at the tender age of eighteen this energetic hooker scored an audacious try against Cardiff under the noses of Terry Holmes, John Scott and Alan Phillips.

Twenty minutes into the England-Wales Twickenham match of 1988 Watkins replaced the injured Kevin Phillips to claim his first cap. He immediately began finding line-out jumper Robert Norster with pin-point accuracy and Welsh fortunes took an upward step along with the quality of their possession.

Watkins also scored a try during his second game for Wales against Scotland at Cardiff a fortnight later.

NEWBRIDGE RFC

HQ: Welfare Ground
Strip: Blue and black hoops

Newbridge's men take the field on turf which owes its smooth contours to the sweat and toil of their forebears.

The club's early history had been nomadic. By the turn of the century they were at their fifth venue, Waen Bedr ('useless area'), which served until 1921. A

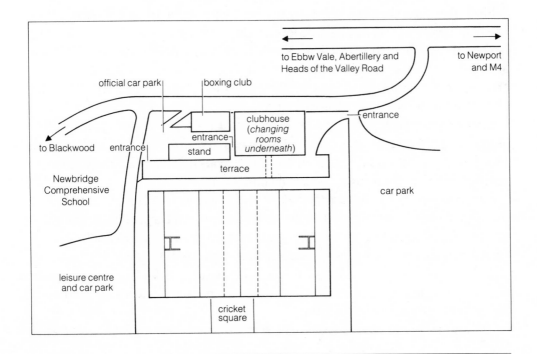

ninety-nine year lease on the present Welfare Ground was then obtained from its owners, the Newbridge and Abercarn Colliery Company. The trouble was that it had been used to dump waste and slurry, and deteriorated into a quagmire at the slightest drop of rain. Staging serious Rugby football on it was initially unthinkable.

In 1925, however, there was a long-drawn-out coal strike. Idle and hard-up miners were only too glad to toil away at removing stones and rubble in exchange for a cup of tea and a packet of cigarettes. Soon a fine playing surface had been achieved – not just for Rugby, for alongside there was now a green field suitable for cricket. A foundation had been laid from which Newbridge could move towards first-class status.

That process still took many years and it was another sad circumstance, the Second World War, which provided the final impetus. Mining had perforce to continue during hostilities; there were enough personnel at the Newbridge collieries to form teams, and matches were played against Cardiff and Newport, who ran wartime sides. After 1945 these links were perpetuated and the club's fixture list expanded rapidly in length and prestige.

In 1961 a major pioneering step was taken and Newbridge became the first club in Wales to accept coaching. Under David Harris' inspiring direction they quickly moved into the top echelon and took the unofficial Championship title in 1964–65 with a style of play that was well-drilled and rehearsed.

Since that time they have been unable to take a major trophy, despite thrice reaching the semi-final of the Schweppes Cup and participating in two Snelling Sevens finals. From time to time, sparked by the brilliant Paul Turner, their entertainment value has been unsurpassed, but achieving consistency has not been easy. For example, in April 1988 their fixtures ended with a 53–10 victory over Ebbw Vale, no fewer than fifty of the points having come in an outstanding second-half display. Just four months later their Centenary season opened with a defeat at the hands of junior rivals Blackwood. By October they had stitched together a sequence of seven fine wins, and it took the Western Samoan tourists to inflict their first home defeat for ten months.

But there are signs of prosperity and high morale at the Welfare Ground. The floodlighting has been improved. A project is underway incorporating a new stand and terrace at the ground's southern end. Former centre Paul Evans has joined Clive Davis to form a formidable coaching axis, with Keith Westwood moving to a managerial role. As chairman, the urbane Mike Croad presides over a happy club, which has struck up a useful and rewarding sponsor relationship with local Japanese electronics company Aiwa.

All Newbridge will wish to guard against is a repeat of the untoward occurrence of 2 October 1975. In the early hours of that morning a hot water cylinder exploded, wrecking the club's reception rooms, bars and changing accommodation. For the remainder of the season teams changed in nearby school buildings.

Newbridge's Great Days

22.2.1982: Newbridge 3pts, Pontypool 0pts

Pontypool have been the most consistent side in Wales for over a decade. Their 1982 Cup run had begun in storming form, and a month before their fourth round appearance at Newbridge they had swept Swansea aside 25–13. Even when they fell behind after three minutes at the Welfare Ground to a Brendan McAloon penalty goal few present seriously thought they would go down to defeat.

Newbridge were without the injured Paul Turner, but his deputy David Owen proceeded to play the game of his life. Harmonising with resilient skipper Lloyd Davies, he nursed his forwards constantly, driving Pontypool back with great line kicking. The home team's reward for a steely display was a first win in four years over their Gwent rivals.

In their first ever semi-final at Rodney Parade a month later Newbridge led eventual Cup winners Cardiff 11–10 at one stage before going out 21–11.

18.10.1983: Newbridge 14pts, Japan 19pts

Japan's visit to Newbridge for their last fixture before the Test against Wales drew a 4000 crowd which saw a thoroughly exciting game. The physically-slight tourists eschewed forward confrontations with burly Welsh opponents in favour of running the ball, and Newbridge chose to play it their way. They thus sacrificed their best chance of winning, but the game was memorable.

Alan Glasson and Martin Short were the try scorers who kept the home team in contention until late in the second half when Japan's stand off half and captain Yuji Matsuo cut through for a third try putting them just out of reach.

15.10.1988: Newbridge 15pts, Western Samoa 16pts

The icing on Newbridge's Centenary cake was the first-ever match between a Welsh club side and Western Samoa. The Welshmen went nine points up within a quarter of an hour through Paul Turner's accurate place-kicking and were threatening to give the tourists a hammering at the tight. Koko and his men, however, fought their way back into contention and scored a pair of scorching tries appreciated by the big crowd. Despite throwing everything into a last desperate bid for victory, Newbridge were thwarted by keen covering and tackling, Western Samoa's defence conceding just one try by Peter Jones which Turner converted.

Newbridge's Heroes

Ray Cale was a ruthless flank forward in the first Welsh post-war Grand Slam side under John Gwilliam. He scored one of the tries in Wales's 1950 win at Twickenham, only her second ever. Piqued, no doubt, at being omitted from the British Lions side which went to New Zealand that summer he promptly signed professional forms for St Helen's Rugby League club.

Don Hayward ranks as the most formidable tight forward produced by Newbridge. He won fifteen caps and played in the Grand Slam sides of 1950 and 1952 before turning professional with Wigan. In due course he emigrated to New Zealand, which he had toured with the British Isles in 1950 (Newbridge's first Lion), and ran a flourishing butcher's business in the busy heart of Wellington.

In 1982 a Newbridge family set an unusual record for Welsh Rugby at Maesteg when father **Dennis Hughes** and his son **Wyn**, a replacement, figured in the same XV. Hughes senior was then forty and had already given twenty-two invaluable years' service to the club.

This Pengam-educated back row man was a tireless forward who began what might have been a long International career against New Zealand in 1967. An ankle injury, however, caused his withdrawal from a Trial a season later, letting in Mervyn Davies to impress the selectors and quickly make the number eight position on his own. Neither Hughes nor any other rival had a look-in for seven years, though the Newbridge man won more caps as a flank forward.

The gifted **Paul Turner** burst upon the scene in 1980 with a record points total of 274. A product of nearby Crumlin, he scored most of his points with the boot – or rather the boots, since he could kick admirably with both feet. In 1983–84 he pushed the total up to 405 (and in a brief spell away from Newbridge set a new Newport record of 368 points in 1986–87).

But Turner will be remembered chiefly as a dazzling runner and handler. For long his approach was too daring and fraught with risk for the Welsh selectors to award him a full cap, and certainly he was sometimes found wanting in judgement. But he was a man whom the crowds loved to watch and applaud – and eventually the Big Five recognised his skills by capping him in 1989.

TREDEGAR RFC

HQ: The Recreation Ground
Strip: Black, red and white hoops

Lesser, though painful, mishaps can befall sports broadcasters than falling from collapsed camera decks (see Llanelli chapter).

At Tredegar one bitterly cold January I was hard at work with my 'lip' microphone, which speakers employ very close to the mouth in order to eliminate

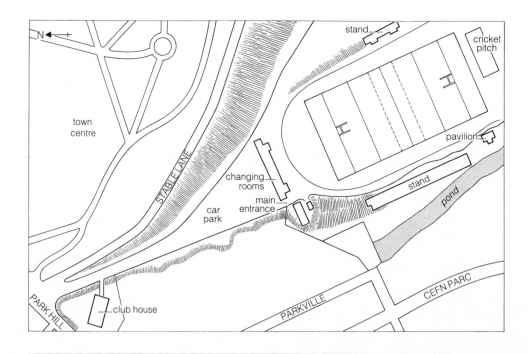

extraneous noise. Even in normal circumstances this piece of equipment rapidly becomes damp with exhaled breath, and the rubber handle which insulates it is often sticky and unpleasant after an hour's continuous use.

On this occasion an exciting passage of Rugby kept me identifying and commentating for close on a minute and a half, an unusually long period of uninterrupted play in the fifteen-a-side game. When a broadcaster finishes a paragraph he removes the microphone from his mouth so that, if necessary, he can talk via the intercom to his director. This I did – in the process peeling off most of my upper lip which had become frozen hard to the steel frame of the instrument! Fortunately the temperature was so low that my ice-bound face felt no pain until later, when first-aid had been applied. Such an experience offers another insight into the so-called glamorous life lived by media folk.

Down in the valley town itself, where Aneurin Bevan was uncrowned king for so long and along whose pavements Michael Foot has stumped in recent years with his trusty stick, all is intimacy and cosiness. The Recreation Ground is laid out on a lofty plateau where in the depths of winter freezing gales bearing frost and snow often gust across the foothills of the Brecon Beacons. It is no place for the faint-hearted; though it goes without saying that the clubhouse welcome in this sector of the Heads of the Valleys area is as warm as the pitch and its surrounds are chill.

With Tredegar RFC our look at the Gwent Connection comes full circle. We are back with manpower problems and a steady exodus – heart-breaking to committee-men and dedicated coaches – of promising young players to other venues. The club have never faltered in their grafting drive towards first-class status, but the task has taken time. After half a century's existence they graduated out of the Monmouthshire League, but in 1950 the only leading sides on their fixture list were the up-and-coming Glamorgan Wanderers and near-neighbours Ebbw Vale. Even now other Gwent sides are granted occasional fixtures against touring sides, and can count on regular matches with Cardiff, neither of which Tredegar have been able to obtain (they once met Cardiff in the Cup and went down to honourable defeat).

However, they can point to heartening progress, and if they have yet to have a player capped from their ranks they have nevertheless enjoyed the services of some accomplished players in recent years, including Wales B lock John Williams, who went to Swansea, and powerful Mark Jones, now of Neath. John Dixon, Peter Bolland, Sid Wharton and Nicky Hunt have injected the necessary quality into their game to bring about good results. These in turn have led to the securing of games against Neath, Newport and Swansea, and after long years spent knocking on the door Tredegar gained admission to the Whitbread Welsh Merit Table group of clubs. Their first full campaign was in 1987–88 when they finished above Penarth and Cross Keys. In October 1988 they met a special Invitation XV in a match to salute the completion of comprehensive ground improvements.

The club play a busy, driving sort of game with few frills, which indirectly led to their figuring in one of the most bizarre occurrences of modern times. Glamorgan Wanderers came to the Recreation Ground for a third round Schweppes Cup tie, oozing confidence after a brilliant unbeaten run of seventeen games dating back to the start of the season. They failed to kick their goals and were bundled out of the competition by fifteen points to twelve, Tredegar's no. eight Chris Evans getting a vital try.

The Wanderers put the cat among the pigeons. They alleged that their conquerors' centre Mark Fowler should not have played, their being doubts about the legality of his transfer from Cilfynydd. Tredegar retorted that this was not the case and that Fowler had been selected in good faith. It took an investigative committee comprising three senior Welsh Rugby Union officers to uphold Tredegar's victory 'in the best interests of the game'.

The Gwent side knocked out Penygraig in the next round before succumbing at home to junior opponents Llanharan.

Tredegar's Great Days

Tredegar's relatively new first-class status means that epic struggles on the grand scale do not figure largely in their annals. However, occasionally they have responded gallantly to the need for a special effort, as when they travelled to play a cup tie against Wrexham in November 1982.

The North Wales champions were full of confidence and ran the ball constantly. Sheer experience, vested in a somewhat elderly pack was the vital factor which saw Tredegar through by 13–12.

Another memorable tussle took place at the Recreation Ground in the third round of the following year's competition. This time it was Tredegar's turn to be optimistic about their chances against Ebbw Vale, having seen off Skewen and Furnace with heavy scoring. The game was postponed for some weeks because of snow lying on the Recreation Ground, and the lay-off perhaps cost Tredegar a few points. They went down by ten points to nine.

THE SUPPORTING CAST

The National XV and the group of top clubs from which International players are normally chosen form the tip of a considerable iceberg. Beginning with mini-Rugby for the very young, it takes in players of literally all shapes, sizes and abilities who wish to run and handle the ball – or simply to shove their weight at a scrummage and knock opponents over with a tackle. Enthusiasm is the raw material; but this must be channelled into a framework which allows men to express themselves – and have fun.

But before examining the base of this structure more closely, let us take account of one or two other clubs which operate at a senior level and, on their day, can achieve parity with any of the Merit Table group. Somewhat on the fringe, for example, but always welcome in the homeland are LONDON WELSH who, after an early nomadic existence, are now well established in permanent headquarters at Old Deer Park. Here, facilities are capacious and sophisticated, with large bars, dining areas and reception rooms; and both visiting contingents and supporters from all over the Home Counties can count on hospitality which is unmistakably Welsh.

The club's fortunes have traditionally depended on the inflow of Welsh 'exiles' seeking employment in the Metropolis. Its profile became sharply defined in the first decade of the twentieth century when its ranks were graced by stars such as Rhys Gabe, Rev John Strand-Jones and E.T. 'Teddy' Morgan who earned immortality by scoring Wales's winning try against the 1905 All Blacks. These were men against whom older-established sides like Blackheath, Harlequins, Cardiff and Newport enjoyed playing, and who helped to make London Welsh a team which would always be welcome back in Wales during the Christmas and Easter holidays.

In their final winter term, Oxbridge Blues not available for the following season have tended to turn to the club for games, and in the 'twenties and 'thirties Harry Bowcott, Wilfred Wooller, Vivian Jenkins and Arthur Rees eagerly made the weekly trip to Town, sometimes linking up with compatriots like Claude Davey or Haydn Tanner. Ronnie Boon and Dick Ellis, both distinguished players, were the reliable administrators who saw the club through the post-war years and the – final – move from Herne Hill to Richmond. They could claim to have laid the foundations of what was one of the most lustrous periods in the history of any Rugby club in the world.

In the 'seventies, coincidence brought together a clutch of enormously gifted players who swept all before them. J.P.R. Williams was studying medicine at St Mary's; Gerald Davies had finished at Cambridge and was teaching in the Home Counties; Jeff Young, Geoff Evans, Mike Roberts, John Taylor and finally Mervyn Davies were London-based. The club sent seven Lions on the historic 1971 tour of Australia and New Zealand – when the British Isles captain was none other than their skipper John Dawes, a laid-back but amazingly effective leader of men with a generous vision of what good Rugby football ought to be. Among the supporting cast were splendid performers like Keith Hughes, Billy Hullin and Jim Shanklin.

Dawes was a kind of supremo at Old Deer Park in those halcyon days (he has a tea-room named after him), and was ably backed by Roger Michaelson and Harry Bowcott. The latter spent a period on the Big Five in the late 'sixties and early 'seventies, when it was said that a couple of gin and tonics pushed along the bar in the great man's direction were an investment that might yield a cap or two; the fact is that Bowcott was an exceptionally shrewd observer of the game who could identify talent before it flowered.

The summit of achievement came in 1972 under Tony Gray, when the Welsh played through a tremendously demanding campaign to capture the Championship title for the first time with a mere six defeats in thirty-six games. Everywhere, they played to packed houses which were never disappointed: the Welsh did not know how to be dull. Frequent successes in the Middlesex Sevens at Twickenham meant that they were the team everyone loved to hate; they took their regular greeting of boos and good-humoured abuse as a compliment.

The dedicated Kevin Bowring kept the club's colours flying in the period following the dissolution of that great side. But at the end of the 'eighties a drying-up of the flow of talent from the homeland has presented a problem – and brought League relegation – since the calibre of first-generation London Welsh recruits has yet to reach a standard that could compensate for this. However, they have a sound base, they have the administrators, they have a glorious history to build on; and their time will come again.

SOUTH WALES POLICE's complex at Waterton Cross is the envy of many rival clubs. The land was bought with commendable foresight shortly after World War II, since which it has grown to stadium proportions. Besides a splendid stretch of turf regularly used by Welsh squads preparing for International matches, there are spacious changing rooms, a big clubhouse, and a sports hall. The Police also stage squash, cricket and soccer matches.

The team's problem is one of continuity, for young, able players drift in and out of the Force's ranks. Since its personnel are drawn from all over the Glamorgan counties, it has also proved unable to attract a loyal sizeable following to fill the ample grandstand.

However, it has made a substantial contribution to the game in Wales in the last decade, when capped players have included Martyn Morris, Richard Donovan, Huw Williams-Jones and the formidable line out forward who joined them from Pontypool, Steve Sutton. Bleddyn Bowen, several times captain of Wales, has certainly been among the most gifted midfield backs of the 'eighties.

The Police have also been fortunate with the quality of their administrators. Until his move to become Secretary of the Welsh Rugby Union, David East spent a decade as Chief Constable and threw his whole weight behind the development of the Rugby club. In Rod Morgan, who died suddenly in the Spring of 1989, they possessed one of the game's most influential men, who had been a hard-working, dedicated national selector in a difficult period for the Welsh game.

CRAWSHAY'S WELSH RFC commemorates the name of its founder, a scion of the great family of ironmasters which dominated heavy industry in the Valleys during the last century. Geoffrey Crawshay, a Welsh Guards officer, established his touring side to foster good fellowship between players and clubs of the Welsh Rugby Union and to encourage young players.

So the present generation of administrators, including Russell Jenkins, Neville Walsh and secretary Terry Flower, call on the stars to carry the name of Welsh Rugby to unlikely venues such as Dubai and Monaco, to play invitation matches against clubs celebrating centenaries, and occasionally to support charitable causes. Along with seasoned players, they select up-and-coming youngsters who benefit from an outing in top company and from the broadening of their Rugby vision. There are also missionary matches against school XVs, when spectators are sometimes rewarded with an enticing glimpse of a genuine golden oldie among all the tearaway teenagers.

Crawshay's are sometimes criticised for contributing to the pressures that Wales's top players experience. They reply vehemently that their fixtures are grouped at the beginning of each season, when players can do with additional match-play, or at its end, when there is less at stake. They are also scrupulous in approaching club committees for permission to select personnel. On balance, their presence adds to the sparkle of the first-class scene.

Another club whose involvement season by season brings freshness and novelty is SOUTH GLAMORGAN INSTITUTE OF HIGHER EDUCATION. Coached and moulded by the indefatigable Leighton Davies, in a vintage winter the students can test the mettle of any senior side. Once known as Cardiff Training College, this establishment boasts among its alumni such giants of the game as Gareth Edwards and John Lloyd, and has traditionally sent out to the clubs young men with a fine understanding of methods and tactics.

Industrial action by schoolmasters in the 'eighties meant that for almost one whole season pupils keen to learn and play Rugby football went untrained and uncoached, and there has been a discernible shudder on what the senior game always saw as a reliable conveyor-belt of well-taught recruits. Nevertheless, the game continues to thrive at the comprehensive – and some junior – schools, and the signs are that many teachers realise more vividly than before how crucial is their input to the health of the game.

Normally caps are awarded at under-fifteen and senior level. Grand Slams prove as elusive as they are at adult level, so that the team of 1983 can look back on their four straight victories as a very special achievement. And in recent years the WELSH SCHOOLS have at least held their own, with victories over France and Scotland and a successful tour of Italy to look back on in 1989. An Under–19 squad who toured New Zealand, however, came back with tails between their legs after a 54–9 defeat in the Test – though they can hardly be said to have fared any worse than the National XV.

The WELSH YOUTH RUGBY UNION, which plays an invaluable role in furthering the careers of boys who leave school at sixteen, have been equally enterprising in spreading their wings. In 1980 they scored one of the most remarkable wins ever registered by any Welsh team of any age-group, defeating South Africa in a 30–25 thriller at Cape Town – the first victory by a representative Welsh side over Springbok opposition. Bleddyn Bowen, Raymond Giles and Terry Shaw were youngsters who, typically, were to make a mark in the senior game.

In the past, however, a long drawn-out interval confronted many players graduating from Schools and Youth ranks before they could realistically bid for further International honours at Wales B level. In the interim, some candidates' appetite for more caps died, or they drifted out of the game. This was the consideration which prompted the WRU to introduce Under-20 and Under-21 teams which now play a series of matches each winter against other countries and student fifteens. Top observers, including the national coach, attend their training sessions to monitor progress, and it is already clear that a useful couple of rungs have been added to the ladder to the top.

Though the elite are watched and snapped up by Merit Table clubs once they mature, for the vast majority of enthusiastic participants in Welsh Rugby future careers are likely to be pursued with the veritable host of District or 'junior' clubs, some of whom are members of the WRU, some of whom are not. From Gwent to Caernarfon, from Pembroke to Clwyd, these really form the loam soil of the game in Wales.

Competition in the Districts is intense and stimulated by a variety of championships and cup competitions. Tumble, for example, have put their name on the map with a sequence of triumphs in the West Wales Rugby Union, which brackets Carmarthenshire and West Glamorgan, capturing the President's Cup five times in succession in the latter part of this decade. Further west there is the prestigious Pembrokeshire Cup to compete for, Tenby arriving at the end of the 'eighties as the dominant side with three successes in four years. The week-in, week-out competition here is what has been known recently as the Jewson Championship. In south-east Wales the 'Silver Ball', the Wrexham Lager Challenge Trophy and the Ben Francis Cup are incentives, while in the north there is the North Wales Cup which go-ahead Wrexham have often captured during the last decade or two.

For non-Union clubs the imaginative Welsh Brewers Cup provides a big stage, bringing together village and suburban sides from all over Wales. It has shone limelight on smaller teams like Blaenavon Forgeside, Bedlinog, Cardiff International AC and Hartridge High School Old Boys. But the glory of Welsh club Rugby is beyond doubt the *SCHWEPPES CUP* Cup tournament, in which the 'minnows' regularly join battle with the biggest fish; and perhaps the best way to pay tribute to the former is to cite ties in which they have forced their more powerful opponents to pull out all the stops – and sometimes won the day.

1972–73, Round 3: Rhymney 9pts, Llanelli 12pts

This was the tie whose final moments the late Carwyn James could not bear to watch. With the eventual Cup-winners trailing 9–6 as injury time began their coach retreated to a quiet corner of the War Memorial ground – from which he heard the cheers, and groans, as Andy Hill escaped Rhymney's clutches for a winning try converted by Phil Bennett.

Rhymney had led through penalty goals by Robert Wood and an Alan Viney dropped goal against Delme Thomas's team. After this battle, senior clubs knew that they could never again take the field against junior opponents in a complacent frame of mind, especially when playing away from home.

1973–74, Round 1: Cardiff HSOB 24pts, Penarth 0pts

My old club enjoyed one of their finest days with this resounding win over Merit Table opponents. The Old Boys, who play on the spacious Diamond Ground (named after a former headmaster) in north Cardiff, were in tremendous form, tries by Vernon Pugh and Andy Holton rocked the Seasiders, and full back Graham Adams sealed their defeat with two conversions and four penalty goals.

Cambridge Blue Gwyn Prescott, with his brother Colin and another man with first-class experience, Ken Roberts, supplied the leavening of experience to see the home side through.

1976–77, Round 3: Tumble 12pts, Newport 12pts

Newport were to win the Schweppes Cup this season for the only time in their history. And before they arrived at hilly Tumble, a village between Carmarthen and Llanelli, they had piled up 124 points in wins over Resolven and Neyland. The locals, however, who can count Wales stand off half Gareth Davies among their more distinguished products, gave the tie their best shot and went out eventually on the ruling which gives victory to the side that scores more tries in the event of a draw. British Lion David Burcher, Newport's captain, got the only one in the game.

1977–78, Round 1: Burry Port 9pts, Swansea 19pts

This tie was a far closer affair than the score-line suggests. The junior side from the coastal district just west of Llanelli fought their way to a 6–6 full-time score – and went into the lead at the start of extra time through a Dennis Lewis penalty.

Swansea pulled themselves together, however, Roger Blyth switching from full back to stand off half in an attempt to bring penetration to the back-line. The move paid off, Roger Davies and Gareth Jenkins scoring tries that put the All Whites on course for an eventual victory in the Final over Newport.

1978–79, Round 2: Ystradgynlais 6pts, Llanelli 6pts

Again, a senior club were saved only by the scoring of a try, in this case by Llanelli scrum half Selwyn Williams whose vital score was converted by Clive Griffiths.

But it was the village side who won all the honours in clinging mud which proved the real leveller. They led the Scarlets for some time through Huw Nicholls' dropped goal and penalty.

1980–81, Round 1: Penclawdd 4pts, Newport 0pts

Penclawdd's victory remains the greatest by a junior club over senior opponents in the Schweppes Cup competition.

A westerly wind howled along the north Gower Coast on this dismal November afternoon, penning mighty Newport near their goal line for long periods in the first half. Here it was that their stand off half, Keith James, fatally delayed a clearance for the villagers' number eight forward Kevin Dallimore to charge his kick down and plunge over for a try that proved decisive.

Though the former Llanelli and Wales B hooker Roy Thomas, who coached Penclawdd, said afterwards that he never thought Newport could get back into the game, he must have had misgivings as his men turned to face the wind. But they held on grimly to reach the second round, only to be dismissed by Neath Athletic.

1984–85, Round 2: Llandovery 21pts, Pontypridd 6pts

Pontypridd's Championship title successes, and their Cup Final appearance, were some years behind them, but they were still expected to deal comfortably with the mid Wales side beneath the shadow of Llandovery's ancient castle.

As it turned out, Ponty were thrown completely out of their stride by the all-out commitment of their smaller opponents, who were shrewdly marshalled by stand off half Carwyn Williams. He landed four penalties, a dropped goal and the conversion of flanker Elfyn Jenkins' opportunist try. There was talk that Llandovery's complement of farmers showed themselves harder on the day than their town-based opponents.

Two other junior clubs scored notable wins on the same day, Seven Sisters winning at Maesteg and Llanharan at Abertillery.

1986–87, Round 3: Cardiff 18pts, Llanharan 14pts

Llanharan, a village on the southern edge of the south Wales coalfield, came close to a shock victory in a thrilling tie at Cardiff Arms Park. Led by former Blue and Black Trevor Worgan, they held a 14–12 advantage over the Cupholders with only five minutes left. Then Gerald Cordle was put away for a long-striding try which Geraint John converted to save the day.

The following year Llanharan showed that their form had been no fluke. They beat Penarth, Gilfach Goch and Tredegar before going down gallantly to Aberavon at the quarter final stage.

1988–89, Round 2: Aberavon Quins 19pts, Aberavon 6pts
Glynneath 15pts, Maesteg 13pts

As the 'eighties drew to a close the junior clubs continued to show that on important days the gap between them and their seniors could be dramatically closed. Aberavon's first defeat at the hands of District opposition came, to their especial chagrin, at the hands of local opponents Aberavon Quins, who took ruthless advantage of the prevailing depression at the Talbot Athletic Ground to win emphatically.

The Quins confined Aberavon to their own 22 for long periods of the cup tie, Keith Davies and John Rees proving an effective half back partnership behind a pack which gave its all. Tries in each half were scored by centre Hugh Williams and back row forward Chris O'Callaghan, full back Michael Jones piling on the agony with three penalties and a conversion.

On the same afternoon, with their number one fan Max Boyce scampering back stage at intervals for news during his pantomime matinee at Cardiff's New Theatre, Glynneath were busy dealing with Maesteg. Here the heroes were centre Robert Jones, with a couple of opportunist tries, and stand off half Phil Evans, who kicked two conversions and a penalty. Maesteg, 15–3 adrift at the break, rallied determinedly in the second half, but with star kicker Jeff Bird off form they could not overhaul the Neath Valley side.

EPILOGUE

In 1945, when I began watching big Rugby, Saturday afternoons were predictable occasions. You bought a programme and took your place on the terrace with a few pals. Out on the pitch a band played. You listened to somewhat inaudible loud-speaker announcements about last-minute team changes. At a minute or so to three o'clock the two teams trotted onto the pitch followed by a referee and touch judges. There were seventy minutes of play to enjoy; after which the teams vanished back beneath the grandstand. End of afternoon out for group of small boys.

Nearly half a century on, that routine has changed little. Here and there taped music has usurped live instrumentalists. There are advertisements to divert the eye, and accommodation has been spruced up. Eighty minutes is now the usual length of a match. Otherwise little is different. Even the publicising and promoting by clubs of fixtures in the Press can hardly be said to have progressed in terms of design and a calculated impact.

Rugby in Wales has been slow to realise that it needs to fight hard for its share of the sporting market. Despite the competing attractions which have made a vigorous challenge in the last couple of decades it remains, with Association Football, a supreme, heart-warming spectacle ideally suited for a winter afternoon's entertainment or exercise. Whatever the older generation may say, it is undoubtedly a better game to watch and to play than was the case fifty years ago – today's score-lines and the number of tries scored underline the point. The clubs, as we have seen, are a colourful ensemble whose players, by and large, retain the capacity to excite and thrill a crowd. But the whole syndrome presents itself indifferently.

Few would argue that the Welsh game should go as far as the version of Rugby played in the United States. But I am firmly of the opinion that more flair should be brought to bear on providing for fans and supporters the kind of atmosphere that cheers the spirit and makes people feel that their presence and encouragement are genuinely sought. A start could be made on match programmes, which are uninspired by comparison with those to be bought at Ninian Park or the Vetch Field. Terse and sketchy club notes fleshed out by bald advertisements are no substitute for the glossy, well-packaged publications bulging with gossip, pen-portraits, statistics and photographs which delight the average football spectator. I often think that the Welsh Rugby Union might put underway some kind of central programme publishing enterprise each Saturday, into an attractive outer brochure individual clubs would then introduce a filling to the 'sandwich', comprising their own team lists, local notes and advertisements.

Clubs and the Welsh Rugby Union might do well to study means of hyping the fixture notices they place in newspapers like the *Western Mail, South Wales Argus* and *Swansea Evening Post.* They have traditionally been able to rely on the appetising copy written by men like J.B.G. Thomas, John Billot, Robin Davey, Ron Griffiths and co to preview matches in an attractive manner. But why not supplement the journalists' efforts by paying for eye-catching advertisements featuring action photographs of match play or studies of star performers due to be on show? Any means of contributing to eager anticipation of a big match, or heightening a potential spectator's feeling that high drama is impending, needs to be exploited.

Many clubhouses in Wales are now very comfortable, welcoming places where members can while away the pre-match period in congenial surroundings and company. Casual spectators, however, are less well catered for. A visit to Gloucester or Bath quickly shows how a well-stocked, efficiently-run, acessible sandwich and drinks counter is appreciated by the fans. Perhaps white-coated popcorn sellers moving along the terraces during play, as in the American superbowls, would be too drastic an innovation. But fans do experience hunger and thirst, especially if they have travelled some distance to attend.

Playing surfaces in mid-winter are often unavoidably sodden and scarcely lend themselves to pre-match parades, displays or even to band concerts. However, thought might be given to some kind of preliminary entertainment which would gradually build up spectators' interest before the kick-off. Even the way players take the field could benefit from some degree of stage-management; many loudspeaker announcers in France name individual participants as they leave the tunnel, thus introducing them to their audience and assisting the public to identify with the actors in the drama. Presentation is the key word.

Why should not players be encouraged to undertake a preliminary canter around the touch-lines before kick-off? This would assist their warm-up and give small boys a chance to wish their heroes good luck. And talking of small boys, who after all will one day be the hulking forwards and quicksilver backs of the future – what ever happened to the complimentary tickets which used to be circulated to local schools when I was a teenager? Watching Bleddyn Williams, Jack Matthews and big Bill

Tamplin for free certainly endeared me and other pupils of Cardiff High School to Cardiff RFC.

The point is that Rugby, and perhaps Welsh Rugby in particular, is a superb product to have on the shelves. But in the era of self-service, help-yourself counters and fast food – and fast sport – windows have to be dressed. For many years the game's administrators found themselves in a sellers' market; but now the paying public is more discerning, and Rugby must adopt new means of getting people through the turnstiles – and persuading the younger generation to take up the game and stay with it. This is the day of the hard sell.

Television in Wales will presumably continue to seek the large audiences it has traditionally attracted for its week-end coverage. But if it desires such a privilege, it too must discover new ways of presenting and portraying the game. For long, BBC Wales was acknowledged as the product-leader in this field: now, though their basic coverage is more erratic, the southern hemisphere's programme-makers have become the innovators – as seizers of half-time interviews, as eavesdroppers upon coaches' pep talks, and as providers of those extra spices that make the main course so appetising.

It is doubtful, too, whether the dismissive quick-cuts from a number of sources and venues now common upon Welsh screens are an adequate substitute for the carefully-edited, longer-drawn-out presentations of bygone days. It is as if the powers-that-be at Broadcasting House in Llandaff have wavered from appreciation of the huge pulling-power good Rugby still has upon its audience, as one of the very few features that can spark the enthusiasm of the Welsh people over a broad front. The BBC pay good money for the privilege of exploiting the game; their reciprocal obligation is to boost it – and there may shortly come a time when a rival challenge will prove more robust and potent to the Welsh Rugby Union as its periodic awarding of the coverage contract is reviewed. HTV makes vigorous noises-off, and has shown ingenuity in importing Rugby tapes from overseas to enthrall its viewers; but without a chance to televise action from domestic games its coverage is inevitably shackled and of less direct relevance to its audience. Many followers of the game would welcome a chance to see what ITV could do if given its head.

It is easy to say that the solutions to all the problems that beset Welsh Rugby football as it surges well into its second century lie in the hands of the Welsh Rugby

Union's top echelon. Certainly it could benefit from a soul-searching review of the way it is comprised and organised. It could inspect its skill at man-management – and ask itself why recent years have been characterised by outbursts of chagrin and frustration from senior International players disenchanted by its attitudes. It should examine its capacity to take initiatives, and to inspire.

But that is too facile. Though the Union is Welsh Rugby's figure-head and, to many, *is* Welsh Rugby, the truth is that Welsh Rugby at large is also the Union. It is for the WRU's myriad component groups and sectors to influence the success and future development of the game in the Principality. They must decide the priorities: whether the game is so valuable that redoubled efforts must be made to seize the young's imagination; whether Welsh Rugby should be simply a wonderful way of letting off steam or a unique shop-window of talent and genius in which victory and national self-respect are vital; whether its top officials and administrators are of satisfactory calibre or need to be replaced by men of greater energy and vision.

For, as in all democracies, the Union's members will get the leadership they deserve. Likewise, Wales will always get the quality of Rugby that it deserves. The twenty-first century waits to see how high that will be.